PHILLIPS' TREASURY OF
HUMOROUS
QUOTATIONS

PHILLIPS' TREASURY OF
HUMOROUS QUOTATIONS

TYNDALE HOUSE PUBLISHERS, INC.
CAROL STREAM, ILLINOIS

BOB PHILLIPS

TYNDALE and Tyndale's quill logo are registered trademarks of Tyndale House Publishers, Inc.

Phillips' Treasury of Humorous Quotations

Designed by Alyssa Force

The unattributed quotes in this book have no verifiable or agreed-upon source.

Library of Congress Cataloging-in-Publication Data

Phillips' treasury of humorous quotations / [compiled by] Bob Phillips.
   p. cm.
ISBN 978-1-4143-0054-2
1. Quotations, English.   2. Wit and humor.   I. Phillips, Bob.
PN6084.H8P48 2004
082'.02'07—dc22   2003025372

ABNORMAL

An abnormal person is anyone who behaves differently from you.

ABORTION

Isn't it funny how everyone in favor of abortion has already been born?
—*Patrick Murray*

ABSENTMINDEDNESS

No man knows what absentmindedness really is until he finds himself dialing his own telephone number.

ABSURDITY

You never know how absurd your own opinion is until you hear somebody else quoting it.

There is no opinion so absurd but that some philosopher will express it.
—*Cicero*

ACCIDENTS

What is better than presence of mind in a railway accident? Absence of body.

If most auto accidents happen within five miles of home, why don't we move ten miles away?
—*Michael Davis*

There would be far fewer accidents if we could only teach telephone poles to be more careful.

Most accidents happen at home—maybe we ought to move.

ACCORDIONS
Accordion: an instrument in harmony with the sentiments of an assassin.
—*Ambrose Bierce*

ACCOUNTANTS
Old accountants never die; they just lose their balance.

ACTING
The most important thing in acting is honesty. If you can fake that, you've got it made.
—*George Burns*

ACTION
A man can do more than he thinks he can, but he usually does less than he thinks he does.

The finest eloquence is that which gets things done.
—*David Lloyd George*

Footprints on the sands of time are not made by sitting down.

As I grow older, I pay less attention to what men say. I just watch what they do.
—*Andrew Carnegie*

ACTIONS

Actions speak louder than words—but not so often.

Actions speak louder than words, and they tell fewer lies.

ACTIVITY

Activity is contagious.
—*Ralph Waldo Emerson*

ACTORS

Never turn your back on an actor; remember, it was an actor who shot Lincoln.

An actor is a man with an infinite capacity for taking praise.

I deny I ever said that actors are cattle. What I said was, "Actors should be treated like cattle."
—*Alfred Hitchcock*

You can pick out the actors by the glazed look that comes into their eyes when the conversation wanders away from themselves.
—*Michael Wilding*

ACTRESSES

The girl who has half a mind to become an actress doesn't realize that's all it requires.

ADAM

Adam was the only man who, when he said a good thing, knew that nobody had said it before him.
—*Mark Twain*

ADAM'S RIB

Adam's rib: the original bone of contention.
—*Oliver Herford and John Clay*

ADOLESCENCE

God's way of making separation with children easier was to invent adolescence.
—*Mark Patinkin*

An adolescent is a teenager who acts like a baby when you don't treat him like an adult.

ADVERSARIES

The rule is perfect: in all matters of opinion our adversaries are insane.
—*Mark Twain*

ADVERSITY

By trying, we can easily learn to reduce adversity—
another man's, I mean.
—*Mark Twain*

Adversity introduces a man to himself.

Adversity makes men wise but not rich.
—*John Ray*

ADVERTISING

The codfish lays ten thousand eggs,
The homely hen lays one.
The codfish never cackles
To tell you what she's done.
And so we scorn the codfish,
While the humble hen we prize,
Which only goes to show you
That it pays to advertise.

ADVICE

Among the many remedies that won't cure a cold,
the most common is advice.

The easiest way to escape being hated is to mind
your own business and refrain from giving good
advice.
—*W. Burton Baldry*

We hate to have some people give us advice because
we know how badly they need it themselves.

We always admire the intelligence of those who ask us for advice.

The best time to give advice to your children is while they're still young enough to believe you know what you're talking about.

Advice is seldom welcome, and those who need it the most like it the least.
—*Lord Chesterfield*

If at first you don't succeed, you'll find everyone giving you advice.

Healthy people have one thing in common: They always give advice to the sick.

When a man seeks your advice, he generally wants your praise.
—*Lord Chesterfield*

When a man comes to me for advice, I find out the kind of advice he wants, and I give it to him.
—*Josh Billings*

How is it possible to expect mankind to take advice when they will not so much as take warning?
—*Jonathan Swift*

Advice is like castor oil, easy enough to give but dreadful uneasy to take.
—*Josh Billings*

If you want people to notice your faults, start giving advice.
—*Kelly Stephens*

Never trust the advice of a man in difficulties.
—*Aesop*

If you want to get rid of somebody, just tell 'em something for their own good.
—*Frank McKinney Hubbard*

AESOP'S FOX
Like Aesop's fox, when he had lost his tail, he would have all his fellow foxes cut off theirs.
—*Robert Burton*

AFFLICTIONS
If afflictions refine some, they consume others.
—*John Ray*

AFTER-DINNER SPEECHES
An after-dinner speech should be like a lady's dress: long enough to cover the subject and short enough to be interesting.

AGE
I think age is a very high price to pay for maturity.

Age is so deceiving. It is amazing how much faster sixty comes after fifty compared to fifty after forty!

When you're over the hill, you pick up speed.

Age is a question of mind over matter. If you don't mind, it doesn't matter.
—*Satchel Paige*

I've reached that age when a good day is one when you get up and nothing hurts.
—*H. Martin*

The years that a woman subtracts from her age are not lost. They are added to the ages of other women.
—*Diane de Poitiers*

I refuse to admit that I am more than fifty-two, even if that does make my sons illegitimate.
—*Nancy Astor*

Age is like love—it cannot be hid.
—*Thomas Dekker*

Age is not a particularly interesting subject. Anyone can get old. All you have to do is live long enough.
—*Groucho Marx*

AGING
The only good thing about [aging] is you're not dead.
—*Lillian Hellman*

The reason mature men look younger than mature women is that a woman of forty is usually fifty.

AGNOSTICS

An agnostic is an irreligious person who stays away from church religiously.

AGREEMENT

Ah, don't say that you agree with me. When people agree with me, I always feel that I must be wrong.
—*Oscar Wilde*

AILMENTS

We are so fond of each other because our ailments are the same.
—*Jonathan Swift*

ALARM CLOCKS

An alarm clock goes off by going on.

An alarm clock is built with a mechanism to scare the daylights into you.

ALGEBRA

Stand firm in your refusal to remain conscious during algebra. In real life, I assure you, there is no such thing as algebra.
—*Fran Lebowitz*

ALLOWANCES
One of the first things a child learns at school is that some other child is getting a bigger allowance.

ALONE
In Genesis it says that it is not good for a man to be alone, but sometimes it is a great relief.
—*John Barrymore*

AMERICA
America is where a young man can start at the bottom and work his way into a hole.
—*Wall Street Journal*

AMERICANS
An American is a man who is proud of his right to say what he pleases and often wishes he had the courage to do so.

[An Englishman is] a person who does things because they have been done before. [An American is] a person who does things because they haven't been done before.
—*Mark Twain*

Americans are getting stronger. Twenty years ago, it took two people to carry ten dollars' worth of groceries. Today, a five-year-old can do it.
—*Henny Youngman*

ANALYSTS

My analyst doesn't understand me.
—*Mel Calman*

ANCESTORS

We pay for the mistakes of our ancestors, and
it seems only fair that they should leave us the
money to pay with.
—*Don Marquis*

ANGELS

Man was created a little lower than the angels and
has been getting a little lower ever since.
—*Josh Billings*

ANGER

Anger makes dull men witty, but it keeps them
poor.
—*Francis Bacon*

Anger begins with madness and ends in regret.

When a man is wrong and won't admit it, he
always gets angry.
—*Thomas Haliburton*

The best way to know a man is to watch him when
he is angry.
—*Hebrew proverb*

When angry, take a lesson from modern science: Always count down before blasting off.

Never go to bed mad. Stay up and fight.
—*Phyllis Diller*

A man's as big as the things that make him mad.

ANIMALS

Animals have these advantages over man: They have no theologians to instruct them, their funerals cost them nothing, and no one starts lawsuits over their wills.
—*Voltaire*

Animals are such agreeable friends—they ask no questions, they pass no criticisms.
—*George Elliot*

ANNOYANCES

I like long walks, especially when they are taken by people who annoy me.
—*Fred Allen*

You do not swear at your serious troubles. One only swears at trifling annoyances.
—*G. F. Turner*

Don't get annoyed if your neighbor plays his stereo at two o'clock in the morning. Call him at four, and tell him how much you enjoyed it.

ANSWERS

He's been that way for years—a born questioner
but he hates answers.
—*Ring Lardner*

ANTAGONISTS

He who wrestles with us strengthens our nerves
and sharpens our skill. Our antagonist is our
helper.
—*Edmund Burke*

ANTICIPATION

If pleasures are greatest in anticipation, remember
that this is also true of trouble.
—*Elbert Hubbard*

ANTS

Which came first—the ant or the picnic?

APARTMENTS

The trouble with modern apartments is that the
walls are too thin when you try to sleep and too
thick when you try to listen.

APPEASERS

An appeaser is one who feeds a crocodile—hoping
it will eat him last.
—*Sir Winston Churchill*

APPENDIXES

If you still have your appendix at middle age, you're probably a surgeon.

It's not true that the appendix is useless; it has put thousands of surgeon's wives in fine furs.

APPLAUSE

My advice to you concerning applause is this: Enjoy it but never quite believe it.
—*Robert Montgomery*

Applause at the beginning of a speech shows the audience has faith; in the middle, it shows their hope; and at the end, their charity.

AQUARIUMS

There is something about a home aquarium that sets my teeth on edge the moment I see it. Why anyone should want to live with a small container of stagnant water populated by a half-dead guppy is beyond me.
—*S. J. Perelman*

ARCHITECTS

The architect makes an old house look better just by talking about the cost of a new one.

ARGUMENTS

There's only one thing worse than the man who will argue over anything, and that's the man who will argue over nothing.

You may easily play a joke on a man who likes to argue—agree with him.
—*Ed Howe*

There are two sides to every argument, and they're usually married to each other.

When you win an argument with your wife, the argument is not over.

I am bound to furnish my antagonists with arguments, but not with comprehension.
—*Benjamin Disraeli*

They are yet but ear-kissing arguments.
—*William Shakespeare*

ARMOR

The best armor is to keep out of range.
—*Italian proverb*

ART

A work of art? It has no invention; it has no order, system, sequence, or result; it has no life likeness, no thrill, no stir, no seeming or reality; its characters are confusedly drawn, and by their acts and words they prove that they are not the sort of people the

author claims that they are; its humor is pathetic; its pathos is funny; its conversations are—oh! indescribable; its love scenes odious, its English a crime against the language. Counting these out, what is left is art. I think we must all admit that.
—*Mark Twain*

ARTISTIC ABILITY
Very few people possess true artistic ability. It is therefore both unseemly and unproductive to irritate the situation by making an effort. If you have a burning, restless urge to write or paint, simply eat something sweet and the feeling will pass.
—*Fran Lebowitz*

ASPIRIN
A rule of thumb in the matter of medical advice is to take everything any doctor says with a grain of aspirin.
—*Goodman Ace*

ASSASSINATION
Assassination is the extreme form of censorship.
—*Bernard Shaw*

ATHEISTS

An atheist is a man who has no invisible means
of support.
—*John Buchan*

An atheist cannot find God for the same reason
a thief cannot find a policeman.

ATHLETE'S FOOT

Before you walk in another guy's boot, make sure
he doesn't have athlete's foot.

ATTICS

An attic is a place where you keep something for
ten years and then throw it away just two weeks
before you need it.

ATTITUDE

We who lived in concentration camps can remember the men who walked through the huts com-
forting others, giving away their last piece of bread.
They may have been few in number, but they offer
sufficient proof that everything can be taken from
a man but one thing: the last of the human free-
doms— to choose one's attitude in any given set
of circumstances, to choose one's own way.
—*Victor E. Frankl*

The man who never does anything he doesn't like
rarely likes anything he does.

The man who doesn't care what others think is generally found at the top of the ladder or at the bottom.

A positive attitude may not solve all your problems but will annoy enough people to make it worth the effort.
—*Herm Albright*

Men are disturbed not by the things that happen but by their opinion of the things that happen.
—*Epictetus*

AUTHORS

Once you've put one of his books down, you simply can't pick it up again.
—*Mark Twain*

If the doctor told me I had only six minutes to live, I'd type a little faster.
—*Isaac Asimov*

What an author likes to write most is his signature on the back of a check.
—*Brendan Francis*

It is part of prudence to thank an author for his book before reading it so as to avoid the necessity of lying about it afterwards.
—*George Santayana*

What an author doesn't know usually fills a book.

AUTHORSHIP
There are three difficulties in authorship: to write anything worth publishing, to find honest men to publish it, and to get sensible men to read it.
—*C. C. Colton*

AVERAGE
Statisticians are men who know that if you put a man's head in a sauna and his feet in a deep freeze, he will feel pretty good—on the average.

If you are average, it means you are as close to the top as you are to the bottom.

Things average out: If you think too much of yourself, others won't.

The trouble with the average man is that he seldom increases his average.

AWARDS
If somebody throws a brick at me, I can catch it and throw it back. But when somebody awards a decoration to me, I am out of words.
—*Harry S. Truman*

AXES
If you'll spend more time sharpening the ax, you'll spend less time chopping wood.

BABES

Out of the mouths of babes comes . . . cereal.

BABIES

Babies do not want to hear about babies; they like
to be told of giants and castles.
—*Samuel Johnson*

The baby wakes up in the wee wee hours of the
morning.
—*Robert Robbins*

There's nothing like having a baby to make you
realize that it's a changing world.

Another thing that has to be learned from the
bottom up is baby care.

A baby is a small creature who soon ceases to be
an armful and grows into quite a handful.

People who say they sleep like a baby usually don't
have one.
—*Leo J. Burke*

When I was born, I was so surprised I didn't talk
for a year and a half.
—*Gracie Allen*

BABY-SITTERS

When you're young, your mother tells you what
time you have to be home; when you're grown up
and married, your baby-sitter tells you.

BABY TALK

Why talk baby talk to an infant when plain
English is hard enough for the poor youngster
to understand?
—*John Kendrick Bangs*

BACHELORS

No one has yet been able to figure out at just what
age a bachelor becomes confirmed.

A bachelor is a man who isn't fit to be tied.

Not every child psychologist is a bachelor, but
every bachelor is a child psychologist.

The difference between a bachelor and a married
man is that one longs for the impossible and the
other has married her.

Bachelors know more about women than
married men. If they didn't, they'd be married,
too.
—*H. L. Mencken*

BACKSEAT DRIVERS
The only motorist who never seems to run out of gas is the backseat driver.

BAD MEMORY
The advantage of a bad memory is that one enjoys several times the same good things for the first time.
—*Friedrich Wilhelm Nietzsche*

BAGPIPES
Bagpipes are the missing link between music and noise.
—*E. K. Kruger*

BALDNESS
One thing about baldness: It's neat.
—*Don Herold*

BALLPARKS
If people don't want to come out to the ballpark, nobody's going to stop them.
—*Yogi Berra*

BALONEY
No matter how thin you slice it, its still baloney.
—*Alfred E. Smith*

BANKERS

[A banker is] a fellow who lends you his umbrella when the sun is shining and wants it back the minute it begins to rain.
—*Mark Twain*

Old bankers never die; they just lose their interest.

BANKRUPTCY

Great is bankruptcy: the great bottomless gulf into which all falsehoods, public and private, do sink, disappearing.
—*Thomas Carlyle*

BARBERS

The world is so confusing nowadays—even your barber has trouble giving you all the answers.

When one barber cuts another barber's hair, which one does the talking?

BARE FEET

He that goes barefoot must not plant thorns.
—*George Herbert*

BARGAINS

On a good bargain think twice.
—*George Herbert*

BASEBALL

Baseball is almost the only orderly thing in a very unorderly world. If you get three strikes, even the best lawyer in the world can't get you off.
—*Bill Veeck*

BASKETBALL PLAYERS

Old basketball players never die; they just dribble away.

BEAR

Tho' the bear be gentle, don't bite him by the nose.
—*Thomas D'Urfey*

BEARBAITING

The Puritans objected to bearbaiting not because it gave pain to the bear but because it gave pleasure to the spectators.
—*Thomas Macaulay*

BEAUTY

I'm tired of all this nonsense about beauty being only skin-deep. That's deep enough. What do you want—an adorable pancreas?
—*Jean Kerr*

Beauty, in a modest woman, is like fire or a sharp sword at a distance: Neither doth the one burn nor the other wound those that come not too near them.
—*Miguel de Cervantes*

BEAUTY PARLORS
When I go to the beauty parlor, I always use the emergency entrance. Sometimes I just go for an estimate.
—*Phyllis Diller*

BEHAVIOR
It is easier to behave your way into a new way of thinking than to think your way into a new way of behaving.

BELIEFS
It doesn't pay well to fight for what we believe in.
—*Lillian Hellman*

BELITTLE
Don't belittle yourself—your friends will do it for you.

BEN HUR
We've got a cat called Ben Hur. We called it Ben till it had kittens.
—*Sally Poplin*

BEST SELLERS

A best seller is usually forgotten within a year, especially by those who borrow it.

BEWARE

Beware of a man who does not talk and a dog that does not bark.
—*Jacob Cats*

BIBLE

A Bible in the hand is worth two on the shelf.

BIGOTS

One who is obstinately attached to an opinion you do not entertain.
—*Ambrose Bierce*

BIG STEP

Don't be afraid to take a big step if one is indicated. You can't cross a chasm in two small jumps.
—*David Lloyd George*

BILLBOARDS

The billboards must go—we need the room for roadside stands, garbage dumps, and auto junkyards.

BIPARTISAN

Whenever a fellow tells me he's bipartisan, I know he's going to vote against me.
—*Harry S. Truman*

BIRD IN THE HAND

A bird in the hand can be messy.

BIRTHDAY CAKES

The woman who puts the right number of candles on her birthday cake is playing with fire.

BLACKMAILERS

A blackmailer is the man who has a skeleton key to the family closet.

BLADDERS

I don't need you to remind me of my age: I have a bladder to do that for me.
—*Stephen Fry*

The length of a film should be directly related to the endurance of the human bladder.
—*Alfred Hitchcock*

BLANKETS

One good turn gets most of the blanket.

BLESSED

Blessed are those who can give without remembering and take without forgetting.
—*Elizabeth Bibesco*

BLIND DATES

When you expect to meet a vision on a blind date, she usually turns out to be a sight.

BLISTERS

If you want a place in the sun, you've got to expect a few blisters.
—*Abigail Van Buren*

BLOCKHEADS

A learned blockhead is a greater blockhead than an ignorant one.
—*Benjamin Franklin*

BLUNDERS

The best time to repent of a blunder is just before the blunder is made.
—*Josh Billings*

BLUSHES

Man is the only animal that blushes, or needs to.
—*Mark Twain*

BOOK REVIEWS

I look upon book reviews as an infantile disease
that newborn books are subject to.
—*G. C. Lichtenberg*

BOOKS

From the moment I picked your book up until the
moment I put it down, I could not stop laughing.
Someday I hope to read it.
—*Groucho Marx*

The covers of this book are too far apart.
—*Ambrose Bierce*

Everything comes to him who waits, except a
loaned book.
—*Frank McKinney Hubbard*

A house without books is like a room without
windows.
—*Horace Mann*

BOREDOM

Boredom, after all, is a form of criticism.
—*William Phillips*

BORES

Talk to a man about himself, and he will listen for
hours.
—*Benjamin Disraeli*

He's the kind of bore who's here today and here
tomorrow.
—*Binnie Barnes*

A bore is a fellow who opens his mouth and puts
his feats in it.
—*Henry Ford*

Bore is too mild a word for some men; they are
more like pneumatic drills.

There are few wild beasts more to be dreaded
than a talking man having nothing to say.
—*Jonathan Swift*

Some men are such bores you can't stand listening
to them even when they're talking about you.

We often forgive those who bore us; we cannot
forgive those whom we bore.
—*François La Rochefoucauld*

BORING
If you haven't struck oil in your first three minutes,
stop boring!
—*George Jessel*

BORROW
Many a man with a big collection of books needs
more shelves but doesn't know how to borrow
shelves.

A person who borrows books becomes his brother's bookkeeper.

BOSSES

The question, "Who ought to be boss?" is like asking, "Who ought to be the tenor in the quartet?" Obviously, the man who can sing tenor.
—*Henry Ford*

You can always tell who the boss is: He's the one who watches the clock during the coffee break.

BOSTON

I have just returned from Boston. It is the only thing to do if you find yourself up there.
—*Fred Allen*

Boston is a moral and intellectual nursery always busy applying first principles to trifles.
—*George Santayana*

BOYS

A good way to get a boy to cut the grass is to forbid him to touch the lawn mower.

It is a mistake to believe that because a boy is quiet, he is up to mischief; he may be asleep.

BRAINS

No diet will remove all the fat from your body because the brain is entirely fat. Without a brain you might look good, but all you could do is run for public office.
—*Covert Bailey*

The human brain starts working the moment you are born and never stops until you stand up to speak in public.
—*George Jessel*

BRAVERY

It is easy to be brave from a safe distance.
—*Aesop*

When you are weaponless, at least act brave.

BREAKFAST

Believe it or not, once upon a time all members of the family had breakfast together.

BREAKS

Night falls but never breaks, and day breaks but never falls.

BUCKS

The buck past before it got here.

BUDGETS

Some couples go over their budgets very carefully every month; others just go over them.
—*Sally Poplin*

BUFFALOES

What really happened to the buffaloes is just what you might expect if you've ever seen one in a zoo—the moths got into them.
—*Will Cuppy*

BUNDLES

Sticks in a bundle are unbreakable.
—*African proverb*

BURDENS

Most families don't want father burdened with money, so they relieve him of his burden.

God gave burdens, also shoulders.
—*Yiddish proverb*

BUREAUCRATS

Old bureaucrats never die; they just waste away.

BURGLARS

Old burglars never die; they just steal away.

BUSINESS

I remember that a wise friend of mine did usually say, "That which is everybody's business is nobody's business."
—*Izaak Walton*

BUSINESSMEN

Of course all boys are not full of tricks, but the best of them are. That is, those who are readiest to play innocent jokes, and who are continually looking for chances to make Rome howl, are the most apt to be first-class businessmen.
—*George W. Peck*

BUSYNESS

Some folks can look so busy doing nothin' that they seem indispensable.
—*Frank McKinney Hubbard*

No one is so busy as the man who has nothing to do.
—*French proverb*

If you want to get a job done, give it to a busy man. The other kind has no time.
—*Elbert Hubbard*

BUYING AND SELLING

I'd like to buy him at my price and sell him at his.

CAB DRIVERS

Cab drivers are living proof that practice does not make perfect.
—*Howard Ogden*

Too bad the only people who know how to run the country are busy driving cabs and cutting hair.
—*George Burns*

CAMELS

A camel never sees its own hump.
—*African proverb*

CANDIDATES

A candidate has to see both sides of an issue— otherwise, how is he going to get around it?

Many a candidate feels that because his rival has been fooling the public for years, he should now be given a chance.

Everyone's talking about how young the candidates are. And it's true. A few months ago Kennedy's mother said, "You have a choice. . . . Do you want to go to camp this year or run for president?"
—*Bob Hope*

CANNIBALS

Is it progress if a cannibal uses knife and fork?
—*Stanislaw J. Lec*

There was an old cannibal whose stomach suffered from so many disorders that he could only digest animals that had no spines. Thus, for years he subsisted only upon university professors.
—*Louis Phillips*

CANNONS
Don't use a cannon to shoot a sparrow.
—*Chinese proverb*

CAPITALISM
The inherent vice of capitalism is the unequal sharing of blessings; the inherent virtue of socialism is the equal sharing of miseries.
—*Winston Churchill*

CAPITAL PUNISHMENT
If you advocate the abolition of capital punishment, remember that you have all the murderers on your side.

CARDS
When a man tells me he's going to put all his cards on the table, I always look up his sleeve.
—*Lord Hore-Belisha*

I must complain the cards are ill shuffled till I have a good hand.
—*Jonathan Swift*

CAREERS

His was the sort of career that made the recording angel think seriously about taking up shorthand.
—*Nicholas Bentley*

CARS

Never lend your car to anyone to whom you have given birth.
—*Erma Bombeck*

Nothing ages your car as much as the sight of your neighbor's new one.

The only thing more disturbing than a neighbor with a noisy old car is a neighbor with a quiet new one.

CASH

Nowadays when a woman furnishes her home in Early American style, it probably means she has paid for it in cash.

Sign in a store: "Cash only, please. We know that your check is good, but we don't trust the banks."

CELEBRITIES

A celebrity is a person who works hard all his life to become well known and then wears dark glasses to avoid being recognized.
—*Fred Allen*

CELLAR DOOR

My parents warned me never to open the cellar door or I would see things I shouldn't see. So one day when they were out, I did open the cellar door, and I did see things I shouldn't see—grass, flowers, the sun.
—*Emo Philips*

CEMETERIES

The fence around a cemetery is foolish, for those inside can't get out, and those outside don't want to get in.

CHANGE

You cannot step twice into the same river, for other waters are continually flowing on.
—*Heraclitus*

In prosperity, prepare for change; in adversity, hope for one.

CHAPERONES

Her face was her chaperone.
—*Rupert Hughes*

CHARACTER

So live that you wouldn't be ashamed to sell the family parrot to the town gossip.
—*Will Rogers*

Character is much easier kept than recovered.
—Thomas Paine

The measure of a man's real character is what he would do if he knew he would never be found out.
—Thomas Babington Macaulay

Character is what you are in the dark.
—Dwight L. Moody

Sow an act, and you reap a habit. Sow a habit, and you reap a character. Sow a character, and you reap a destiny.
—Charles Reade

Underneath this flabby exterior is an enormous lack of character.
—Oscar Levant

A pat on the back will build character if applied low enough, hard enough, and often enough.

No man knows his true character until he has run out of gas, purchased something on the installment plan, and raised an adolescent.
—Mercelene Cox

CHARITY

Charity begins at home and generally dies from lack of outdoor exercise.

When it comes to giving charity, some people stop at nothing.

CHARMERS

Do you know the difference between a beautiful woman and a charming one? A beauty is a woman you notice; a charmer is one who notices you.
—*Adlai Stevenson*

CHEER

The best way to cheer yourself up is to try to cheer somebody else up.
—*Mark Twain*

CHEERFULNESS

Early morning cheerfulness can be extremely obnoxious.
—*William Feather*

CHEESE

How can you be expected to govern a country that has 246 kinds of cheese?
—*Charles de Gaulle*

Poets have been mysteriously silent on the subject of cheese.
—*G. K. Chesterton*

CHESS

Life's too short for chess.
—*Henry James Byron*

CHILD

Teach your child to hold his tongue; he'll learn fast enough to speak.
—*Benjamin Franklin*

Nothing annoys the average child today like a disobedient parent.

Ask your child what he wants for dinner only if he's buying.
—*Fran Lebowitz*

Many kiss the child for the nurse's sake.
—*John Heywood*

CHILD PSYCHOLOGY

Child psychology has discovered many excellent rules for bringing up other people's children.

CHILDREN

It's really unbelievable how many mistakes the neighbors can make in raising their children.

Grown-ups never understand anything for themselves, and it is tiresome for children to be always and forever explaining things to them.
—*Antoine de Saint-Exupéry*

Oh, what a tangled web do parents weave when they think that their children are naïve.
—*Ogden Nash*

Small children constantly play on your emotions: They are either a lump in the throat or a pain in the neck.

Children are natural mimics who act like their parents in spite of every effort to teach them good manners.

The value of marriage is not that adults produce children but that children produce adults.
—*Peter de Vries*

Children keep a family together, especially when one can't get a baby-sitter.

No wonder it's so difficult to raise children properly— they are always imitating their parents.

Some people can trace their ancestry back hundreds of years but cannot tell you where their children were last night.

The best way to keep children home is to make the home atmosphere pleasant and let the air out of the tires.
—*Dorothy Parker*

When a father doesn't have the upper hand with his children, it is usually because he has failed to lower his.

The thing that impresses me most about America is the way parents obey their children.
—*Duke of Windsor*

Parents are embarrassed when their children tell lies—and even more embarrassed when they tell the truth.

Two of anything but children make a pair; two of them make a mob.

I know a lot about children. Not being an author, I'm a great critic.
—*Finley Peter Dunne*

Child guidance is what parents get from their children nowadays.

Man is lazy by nature, so God gave us children to get us up early.
—*Henny Youngman*

Children really brighten up a household—they never turn the lights off.
—*Ralph Bus*

Each day of our lives we make deposits in the memory banks of our children.
—*Charles R. Swindoll*

The persons hardest to convince they're at the retirement age are children at bedtime.
—*Shannon Fife*

Before I was married I had three theories about raising children. Now I have three children and no theories.
—*John Wilmot*

Children today are tyrants. They contradict their parents, gobble their food, and tyrannize their teachers.
—*Socrates*

If you don't want your children to hear what you are saying, pretend you're talking to them.

Children are unpredictable. You never know what inconsistency they're going to catch you in next.
—*Franklin P. Adams*

You can do anything with children if you only play with them.
—*Otto von Bismarck*

CHINESE FOOD

You do not sew with a fork, and I see no reason why you should eat with knitting needles.
—*Miss Piggy*

When it comes to Chinese food, the less known about the preparation the better.
—*Calvin Trillin*

CHIP ON THE SHOULDER

One of the heaviest burdens a person can carry is a chip on his shoulder.
—*Olin Miller*

A chip on the shoulder is too heavy a piece of
baggage to carry through life.
—*B. C. Forbes*

Don't go around with a chip on your shoulder;
people might think it came off your head.

CHOPS

Chop: A piece of leather skillfully attached to
a bone and administered to the patients at
restaurants.
—*Ambrose Bierce*

CHRISTIANS

Going to church doesn't make you a Christian any
more than going to the garage makes you a car.
—*Laurence Peter*

CHRYSANTHEMUMS

A chrysanthemum by any other name would be
easier to spell.
—*William J. Johnston*

CHURCH

A great many more men would want to go to
church if there were a law against it.

If all the people who sleep in church were placed
end to end, they would be more comfortable.

Don't stay away from church because there are so many hypocrites. There's always room for one more.
—*A. R. Adams*

CIVILIZATION
The three principal things that hold civilization together are the safety pin, the paper clip, and the zipper.

CIVIL SERVICE
The man who never worries or hurries is probably in civil service.

"CLAIR DE LUNE"
I only know two pieces: One is "Clair de Lune," and the other one isn't.
—*Victor Borge*

CLASSICAL MUSIC
Classical music is music written by famous dead foreigners.
—*Arlene Heath*

CLASSICS
A classic is something that everybody wants to have read and nobody wants to read.
—*Mark Twain*

CLAUSTROPHOBIA

Claustrophobia? It's a dreadful fear of Santa Claus.
—*Vinnie Barbarino*

CLEANING

Cleaning your house while your kids are still growing is like shoveling the walk before it stops snowing.
—*Phyllis Diller*

CLEVERNESS

It is very clever to know how to hide one's cleverness.
—*François La Rochefoucauld*

He might be a very clever man by nature for all I know, but he laid so many books upon his head that his brains could not move.
—*Robert Hall*

When a wife laughs at her husband's jokes, it's not because they are clever, but because she is.

I always did think that cleverness was the art of hiding ignorance.
—*Shelland Bradley*

CLOCK WATCHERS

An office clock is rarely stolen—probably because everyone watches it.

Some of the laziest people I know are the world's best clock watchers.

CLOSETS
The last place people want to hang clothes is their clothes closet. Closets are mean, inconvenient, often dark, and always overcrowded. If a person's closet isn't overcrowded, you can bet that person needs a psychiatrist.
—*Andy Rooney*

CLOTHES
Clothes make the man. Naked people have little or no influence on society.
—*Mark Twain*

CLUTTERED
If a cluttered desk is the sign of a cluttered mind, what is the significance of a clean desk?
—*Laurence J. Peter*

COFFEE
If this is coffee, please bring me some tea; but if this is tea, please bring me some coffee.
—*Abraham Lincoln*

COFFEE BREAKS
Do the employees at a tea factory get a coffee break?

In some government offices there are so many coffee breaks that the employees can't sleep at their work.

COLD FEET

Some are born with cold feet, some acquire cold feet, and others have cold feet thrust upon them.

COLDS

Why is it that only people who are not doctors know how to cure a cold?

COLLEGE

Another thing that a young man learns at college is that he's terribly short of money.

College football players seldom have trouble with running and kicking but often have trouble with passing.

Many a man who spends thousands of dollars on his son's college education gets only a quarter back.

Some students take up the arts in college, some take up the sciences, while others just take up space.

COLLEGE PRESIDENTS

Old college presidents never die; they just lose their faculties.

COME AGAIN

You must come again when you have less time.
—*Walter Sickert*

COMIC STRIPS

There are more comic strips on the beaches than in the newspapers.

COMMITMENT

With regard to ham and eggs: The chicken is involved; the pig is committed.
—*Abraham Lincoln*

COMMITTEES

A committee is a group that keeps minutes and loses hours.
—*Milton Berle*

What is a committee? A group of the unwilling, picked from the unfit, to do the unnecessary.
—*Richard Harkness*

Committees have become so important nowadays that subcommittees have to be appointed to do the work.
—*Laurence J. Peter*

COMMON-LOOKING PEOPLE

The Lord prefers common-looking people. That is the reason he makes so many of them.
—*Abraham Lincoln*

COMMON SENSE

Another thing this country needs is a college that gives a degree in common sense.

Nothing astonishes men so much as common sense and plain dealing.
—*Ralph Waldo Emerson*

COMMUNISTS

What is a Communist? One who has yearnings for equal division of unequal earnings.
—*Ebenezer Elliot*

A Communist is one who has nothing and is eager to share it with others.

If the Communists worked just as hard as they talked, they'd have the most prosperous style of government in the world.
—*Will Rogers*

COMPANY

A man is known by the company he keeps out of.
—*A. Craig*

COMPASSION

Compassion will cure more sins than condemnation.
—*Henry Ward Beecher*

COMPLIMENTS

Some people pay a compliment as if they expected a receipt.
—*Frank McKinney Hubbard*

I can live for two months on a good compliment.
—*Mark Twain*

COMPUTERS

To err is human, but to really foul things up requires a computer.

CONCEIT

Conceit is a strange disease; it makes everyone sick except the person who has it.

The world tolerates conceit from those who are successful but not from anybody else.
—*John Blake*

Conceit is God's gift to little men.
—*Bruce Barton*

CONCENTRATION

When a man knows he is to be hanged in a fortnight, it concentrates his mind wonderfully.
—*Samuel Johnson*

CONCILIATION

An infallible method of conciliating a tiger is to allow oneself to be devoured.
—*Konrad Adenauer*

CONCLUSIONS

Jumping to conclusions seldom leads to happy landings.

Some people exercise by jumping to conclusions, some by sidestepping their responsibilities, but most people get it by running down their friends.

CONFERENCES

A conference is a gathering of important people who singly can do nothing but together can decide that nothing can be done.
—*Fred Allen*

CONFESSION

Nothing spoils a confession like repentance.
—*Anatole France*

CONFIDENCE

Confidence is that quiet, assured feeling you get just before you fall flat on your face.

CONFUSION

If you're not confused, you're not paying attention.

CONGRESS

Tomorrow is Labor Day, I suppose set by act of Congress. How Congress knows anything about labor is beyond me.
—*Will Rogers*

Congressional terms should be . . . ten to twenty with no possibility of parole.
—*Walt Handelsman*

When a man runs for Congress, you're a friend; when he's elected, you're a constituent; when he's legislating, you're a taxpayer.

The attitude of Congress toward hidden taxes is not to do away with them but just to hide them better.

Think of what would happen to us in America if there were no humorists—life would be one long *Congressional Record.*
—*Thomas L. Masson*

All Congresses and Parliaments have a kindly feeling for idiots and a compassion for them on account of personal experience and heredity.
—*Mark Twain*

CONSCIENCE

Conscience: That which makes a boy tell his mother before his sister does.
—*Laurence J. Peter*

Conscience is the inner voice that warns us that someone may be looking.
—*H. L. Mencken*

Removing a man's conscience is usually just a minor operation.
—*Jesse S. Jones*

Conscience is the playback of the still, small voice that warned you not to do it in the first place.

Conscience is a cur that will let you get past it but that you cannot keep from barking.

I have noticed my conscience for many years, and I know it is more trouble and bother to me than anything else I started with.
—*Mark Twain*

CONTEMPT

Silent contempt is the noblest way a man can express himself when the other fellow is bigger.

CONTENTMENT

Who is rich? He who is content. Who is that? Nobody.

The contented man is never poor; the discontented man is never rich.

CONTRADICTIONS

A man never tells you anything until you contradict him.
—*Bernard Shaw*

CONTRARINESS

Some folks are so contrary that if they fell in a river, they'd insist on floating upstream.
—*Josh Billings*

CONVERSATION

Conversation would be vastly improved by the constant use of four simple words: I do not know.
—*André Maurois*

The art of conversation is not knowing what you ought to say but what one ought not to say.

There are two faults in conversation, which appear very different, yet arise from the same root and are equally blameable: I mean an impatience to interrupt others and the uneasiness of being interrupted ourselves.
—*Jonathan Swift*

Cutting in on some conversation is about as easy as threading a sewing machine needle when it is operating at full speed.
—*Ray Pierce*

COOKING DINNER
There is no spectacle on earth more appealing than that of a beautiful woman in the act of cooking dinner for someone she loves.
—*Thomas Wolfe*

CORPORATIONS
Corporation: an ingenious device for obtaining individual profit without individual responsibility.
—*Ambrose Bierce*

COURAGE
He has all the courage of a lame mouse in a lion's cage.
—*Jim Bishop*

COURTSHIP
In a courtship the heart beats so loudly it blocks out the sound from the mind.
—*Bern Williams*

CRAFTINESS

Craftiness must have clothes, but truth loves to go naked.

CRAZY

If I wanted to go crazy, I would do it in Washington because it would not be noticed.
—*Irwin S. Cobb*

CREDIT

Credit: what you use to buy today what you can't afford tomorrow while you're still paying for it yesterday.

Next to the man who invented taxes, the one who caused the most trouble in the world is the man who invented credit.

Credit is a clever financial trick that enables us to spend what we haven't got.

Many a man who seems to be on Easy Street is only on Easy Payment Plan.

CREDIT CARDS

A credit card sometimes adds to the high cost of living but more often to the cost of high living.

You can pay for everything nowadays with a credit card—except the monthly bills you run up with it.

CREDITORS

Running into debt isn't so bad. It's running into creditors that hurts.
—*Jacob M. Braude*

CRICKET

Cricket is a game that the British, not being a spiritual people, had to invent in order to have some concept of eternity.
—*Lord Mancroft*

CRISES

There cannot be a crisis next week. My schedule is already full.
—*Henry Kissinger*

CRITICISM

To escape criticism—do nothing, say nothing, be nothing.
—*Elbert Hubbard*

If criticism had any real power to harm, the skunk would have been extinct by now.
—*Fred Allen*

Honest criticism is hard to take, particularly from a relative, a friend, an acquaintance, or a stranger.
—*Franklin P. Jones*

CRITICS

A critic is a legless man who teaches running.
—*Channing Pollock*

A critic is a gong at a railroad crossing clanging
loudly and vainly as the train goes by.
—*Christopher Morley*

Critics are a dissembling, dishonest, contempt-
ible race of men. Asking a working writer what he
thinks about critics is like asking a lamppost what
it feels about dogs.
—*John Osborne*

CROCODILES

Don't think there are no crocodiles just because
the water is calm.

CROWDS

Every crowd has a silver lining.
—*P. T. Barnum*

CRYING

Smile and the world smiles with you; cry and you
get a red nose.

CUCUMBERS

A cucumber should be well sliced and dressed

with pepper and vinegar and then thrown out, as good for nothing.
—*Samuel Johnson*

CUSTARD

Custard: a detestable substance produced by a malevolent conspiracy of the hen, the cow, and the cook.
—*Ambrose Bierce*

CUSTOMS

Have a place for everything and keep the thing somewhere else; this is not advice, it is merely custom.
—*Mark Twain*

CYNICS

A cynic is a man who, when he smells flowers, looks around for a coffin.
—*H. L. Mencken*

"DARLING"

Darling: the popular form of address used in speaking to a member of the opposite sex whose name you cannot at the moment remember.
—*Oliver Herford*

DEAFNESS

No one is as deaf as the man who will not listen.

DEATH

Death: to stop sinning suddenly.
—*Elbert Hubbard*

He who would teach men to die would teach them to live.
—*Michel de Montaigne*

DEBT

Nothing gets you into debt faster than trying to keep up with people who are already there.

He that dies pays all debts.
—*William Shakespeare*

DECISIONS

Wherever you see a successful business, someone once made a courageous decision.
—*Peter Drucker*

A decision is what a man makes when he can't get anyone to serve on a committee.
—*Fletcher Knebel*

DEEDS
Talk is cheap; actions are gold.

DEMOCRACY
Democracy is the worst form of government, except for all the other forms that have already been tried.

Democracy is a process by which the people are free to choose the man who will get the blame.

In a democracy you can speak your mind; the only difficulty is to get someone to listen.

Democracy is a form of government where you can say what you think even if you don't think.

DEMOCRATS
I am not a member of any organized party—I am a Democrat.
—*Will Rogers*

I never said all Democrats were saloonkeepers. What I said was that all saloonkeepers are Democrats.
—*Horace Greeley*

DENIAL

Never believe anything until it has been officially denied.
—*Claud Cockburn*

DEPRESSION

He's turned his life around. He used to be depressed and miserable. Now he's miserable and depressed.
—*David Frost*

Noble deeds and hot baths are the best cures for depression.
—*Dodie Smith*

DEVIL

Wherever God erects a house of prayer,
The Devil always builds a chapel there;
And 'twill be found, upon examination,
The latter has the largest congregation.
—*Daniel Defoe*

We have done away with the devil these days because man can now be trusted to carry on the work himself.

Some people sell themselves to the devil; others rent themselves out by the day.

DIAGNOSIS

The doctor asks the patient what's wrong, and then the patient asks the doctor.

DIAMONDS

A box of candy means friendship, a bunch of flowers means love, but a diamond means business.

The diamond is the hardest stone . . . to get.

Let us not be too particular; it is better to have old, secondhand diamonds than none at all.
—*Mark Twain*

DICE

The best throw with the dice is to throw them away.

DICTATORS

Dictators believe in only one liberty—the liberty to do away with all the other liberties.

DIETS

I've been on a diet for two weeks, and all I've lost is two weeks.
—*Totie Fields*

The worst thing about a reducing diet is not watching your food but watching everyone else's.

What's the use of going on a diet on which you starve to death just to live longer?

Probably nothing in the world arouses more false hopes than the first four hours of a diet.
—*Dan Bennett*

DIFFERENCES
The difference between us and other people is that their money looks bigger and their troubles smaller.

DIMPLES
Many a man in love with a dimple makes the mistake of marrying the whole girl.
—*Stephen Leacock*

DINNER PARTIES
At a dinner party we should eat wisely but not too well and talk well but not too wisely.
—*Somerset Maugham*

DIPLOMACY
Diplomacy is the art of saying "nice doggie" until you can find a rock.
—*Will Rogers*

Diplomacy: lying in state.
—*Oliver Herford*

Diplomacy is the art of keeping your shirt on while you are getting something off your chest.

You take diplomacy out of war, and the thing would fall flat in a week.
—*Will Rogers*

DIPLOMATS

A diplomat is a man who always remembers a woman's birthday but never remembers her age.
—*Robert Frost*

In order to be a diplomat, one must speak a number of languages, including doubletalk.
—*Carey Williams*

Diplomats are just as essential to starting a war as soldiers are for finishing it.
—*Will Rogers*

DISAGREEMENTS

In our home we have a rule: You can disagree with a man's position as much as you want—after you have been able to state it to his satisfaction.
—*J. Irwin Miller*

We're having a little disagreement. What I want is a big church wedding with bridesmaids and flowers and a no-expense-spared reception, and what he wants is to break off our engagement.
—*Sally Poplin*

DISAPPOINTMENTS

The biggest disappointments come to those who get what's coming to them.

DISCIPLINE

Every child should have an occasional pat on the back as long as it is applied low enough and hard enough.
—Bishop Fulton J. Sheen

DISCOVERY

Man cannot discover new oceans until he has courage to lose sight of the shore.

DISCRETION

More trouble is caused in the world by indiscreet answers than by indiscreet questions.
—Sydney J. Harris

The trouble with discretion is that it usually comes too late to do any good.

DISORDERLINESS

One of the advantages of being disorderly is that one is constantly making exciting discoveries.
—A. A. Milne

DIVORCE

Divorce is so common that some couples stay
married just to be different.

DOCTORS

The doctor felt the man's purse and said there
was no hope.

Nobody wants to be married to a doctor who
works weekends and makes house calls at 2 A.M.
But every patient would like to find one.
—*Ellen Goodman*

Never go to a doctor whose office plants are dead.
—*Erma Bombeck*

Doctors think a lot of patients are cured who have
simply quit in disgust.
—*Don Herold*

It is a good idea to "shop around" before you
settle on a doctor. Ask about the condition of
his Mercedes. Ask about the competence of his
mechanic. Don't be shy! After all, you're paying
for it.
—*Dave Barry*

My doctor is so busy—while in his waiting room
I caught another disease.

When a patient is at death's door, it is the duty of
his doctor to pull him through.

A doctor is a general practitioner who calls in a specialist to share the blame.

Doctors are just the same as lawyers; the only difference is that lawyers merely rob you, whereas doctors rob you and kill you, too.
—*Anton Chekhov*

DO UNTO OTHERS

Do not do unto others as you would have them do unto you—their tastes might not be the same.
—*George Bernard Shaw*

DOGMATISM

When people are least sure, they are often more dogmatic.
—*J. K. Galbraith*

Dogmatism: that wretched disease that rivets a man so firmly to his own belief that he becomes incapable of conceiving other men may believe otherwise.
—*Michel de Montaigne*

DOGS

I broke our dog from begging for food from the table. I let him taste it.

A dog is the only thing on earth that loves you more than you love yourself.
—*Josh Billings*

If a dog could talk, he wouldn't be man's best friend for long.

A dog teaches a body fidelity, perseverance, and to turn 'round three times before lying down.
—*Robert Benchley*

If you pick up a starving dog and make him prosperous, he will not bite you; that is the principal difference between a dog and a man.
—*Mark Twain*

Every boy who has a dog should also have a mother so the dog can be fed regularly.

I have always liked bird dogs better than kennel-fed dogs myself—you know, one that will get out and hunt for food rather than sit on his fanny and yell.
—*Charles E. Wilson*

Outside of a dog, a book is man's best friend. Inside of a dog, it's too dark to read.
—*Groucho Marx*

He has all the characteristics of a dog—except loyalty.
—*Sam Houston*

DONKEYS

Until the donkey tried to clear the fence, he
thought himself a deer.
—*Arthur Guiterman*

Cropping a donkey's ears will not produce a stallion.

DO-NOTHINGS

He did nothing in particular and did it very well.
—*W. S. Gilbert*

DOWNCAST

A good way to perk up your spirits whenever
you're downcast is to think back over the persons
you might have married.

DREAM HOUSE

The trouble with a dream house is that it costs
twice as much as you dreamed it would.

DRESSMAKERS

Good often comes from evil: the apple that Eve
ate has given work to thousands of designers and
dressmakers.

DRIVERS

It is untrue that Germans are bad drivers. They hit
everything they aim at.
—*Joey Adams*

DRIVEWAYS

We drive on a parkway but park in a driveway.

DRIVING

Nothing improves a man's driving like being followed by a police car.

If your wife wants to learn to drive, don't stand in her way.
—*Sam Levenson*

DROPOUTS

Another way to solve the school dropout problem is to make a high school diploma a prerequisite for a driver's license.

DRUMS

The first thing a child learns after he gets a drum is that he's never going to get another.

DRUNKS

Let him who sins when drunk be punished when sober.

DULLNESS

The town was so dull that when the tide went out, it refused to come back.
—*Fred Allen*

DUMB

Dumb enough to chew on the stick instead of sucking the lollipop.
—*Rex Stout*

While he was not as dumb as an ox, he was not any smarter either.
—*James Thurber*

DUMB QUESTIONS

Asking dumb questions is easier than correcting dumb mistakes.

DUTY

The best way to get rid of your duties is to discharge them.

When a stupid man is doing something he is ashamed of, he always declares that it is his duty.
—*George Bernard Shaw*

Happiness is the natural flower of duty.
—*Phillips Brooks*

Do something every day that you don't want to do; this is the golden rule for acquiring the habit of doing your duty without pain.
—*Mark Twain*

EARLY

Being early is an unpardonable sin. If you are early, you'll witness the last-minute confusion and panic that always attend making anything seem effortlessly gracious. Looking in on this scene is almost as rude as asking someone where he got his face-lift.
—*P. J. O'Rourke*

Early to bed and early to rise is a sure sign that you're fed up with television.
—*Henny Youngman*

EARS

The eyes believe themselves; the ears believe other people.

Nature has given men one tongue but two ears that we may hear from others twice as much as we speak.
—*Epictetus*

EARTH

Earth here is so kind, that just tickle her with a hoe, and she laughs with a harvest.
—*Douglas Jerrold*

EATING

Never eat more than you can lift.
—*Miss Piggy*

Children are always being told to eat more by parents who are always being told to eat less.

EATING CROW

Food isn't the only thing that causes indigestion: You can also get it from eating crow and swallowing your pride.

ECHOES

Don't be an echo; remember, though it's always an exact imitation, it never contributes anything new.

ECONOMISTS

If all the nation's economists were laid end to end, they would point in all directions.

If all economists were laid end to end, they would not reach a conclusion.
—*George Bernard Shaw*

ECONOMY

It is remarkable how little a man can live on, especially when compared with how much he wants.

EDUCATION

They say that we are better educated than our parents' generation. What they mean is that we go to school longer. They are not the same thing.
—*Douglas Yates*

He was so learned that he could name a horse in nine languages; so ignorant that he bought a cow to ride on.
—*Benjamin Franklin*

Education is something you get when your father sends you to college. But it isn't complete until you send your son there.

Nothing in education is so astonishing as the amount of ignorance it accumulates in the form of inert facts.
—*Henry Adams*

If a man empties his purse into his head, no one can take it from him.
—*Benjamin Franklin*

If you think education is expensive, try ignorance.
—*Derek Bok*

Of what use is a college education to high school graduates who already know everything?

Another way to get an education is to drive a school bus.

Sixty years ago I knew everything; now I know nothing; education is a progressive discovery of our own ignorance.
—*Will Durant*

EFFICIENCY EXPERTS
An efficiency expert is one who waits to make up a foursome before going through a revolving door.

EFFORT
Everything requires effort; the only thing you can achieve without it is failure.

EGGS
Put all your eggs in one basket—and watch the basket.
—*Mark Twain*

EGOTISTS
When an egotist gets up in the morning and puts his pants on, he thinks the whole world is dressed.

Give the egotist his due; he never goes around talking about other people.

ELEPHANTS
They say the elephant never forgets, but what has he got to remember?

I have a memory like an elephant. In fact, elephants often consult me.
—*Noel Coward*

When you have got an elephant by the hind legs and he is trying to run away, it's best to let him run.
—*Abraham Lincoln*

EMPTINESS

People who would think of talking with their mouths full often speak with their heads empty.

The empty cask makes the most sound.
—*Jacob Cats*

EMPTY POCKETS

The devil dances in an empty pocket.

END OF YOUR ROPE

When you get to the end of your rope, tie a knot and hang on.
—*Franklin D. Roosevelt*

ENDS MEET

Just about the time you think you can make both ends meet, somebody comes along and moves the ends.

ENDURANCE

Never mistake endurance for hospitality.

ENEMIES

The Bible tells us to love our neighbors and also to love our enemies—probably because they are generally the same people.
—*G. K. Chesterton*

Don't bore your friends with your troubles; tell them to your enemies—they'll enjoy hearing about them.

I'm lonesome. They are all dying. I have hardly a warm personal enemy left.
—*J. A. McNeill Whistler*

Bernard Shaw is an excellent man; he has not an enemy in the world, and none of his friends like him.
—*Oscar Wilde*

To have a good enemy, choose a friend—he knows best where to stick the knife.

If you really want to annoy your enemy, keep silent and leave him alone.

ENGLAND

In order to appreciate England one has to have a certain contempt for logic.
—*Lin Yutang*

The best thing I know between France and England is the sea.
—*Douglas Jerrold*

ENOUGH

Nothing is enough for the man to whom enough is too little.
—*Epicurus*

ENTHUSIASM

The employee who is fired with enthusiasm is seldom fired.

ENVY

It is the practice of the multitude to bark at eminent men, as little dogs do at strangers.
—*Seneca*

EXPERIENCE

Knowledge is what you get from reading the small print in a contract; experience is what you get from not reading it.

Experience teaches you that the man who looks you straight in the eye is hiding something, particularly if he adds a firm handshake.
—*Clifton Fadiman*

FACES

As a beauty I'm not a great star.
There are others more handsome, by far,
But my face—I don't mind it
Because I am behind it;
It's the people in front get the jar.
—Anthony Euwer

He had the sort of face that once seen is never remembered.
—Oscar Wilde

Another way in which a woman loses face is by misplacing her cosmetic kit.

FACTS

Get your facts first, and then you can distort them as much as you please.
—Mark Twain

FAILINGS

People in general will much better bear being told their vices and crimes than of their failings and weaknesses.
—Lord Chesterfield

FAILURES

Failure has gone to his head.
—Wilson Mizner

I cannot give you the formula for success, but
I can give you the formula for failure—which is:
Try to please everybody.
—*Herbert Bayard Swope*

Half the failures in life arise from pulling in one's
horse as he is leaping.
—*J. C. and A. W. Hare*

FAITH
'Tis not the dying for a faith that's so hard . . .
every man of every nation has done that—'tis the
living up to it that's difficult.
—*William Makepeace Thackeray*

FAME
Fame is the perfume of heroic deeds.
—*Socrates*

The fame of great men ought to be judged always
by the means they used to acquire it.
—*François La Rochefoucauld*

FAMILIARITY
Familiarity breeds contempt—and children.
—*Mark Twain*

FAMILY

Nowadays two can live as cheaply as one large family used to!
—*Joey Adams*

I come from a wealthy family. My brother is worth fifty thousand dollars—dead or alive.

FAMILY TREE

Why pay money to have your family tree traced; just go into politics, and your opponents will do it for you.

I don't have to look up my family tree because I know that I'm the sap.
—*Fred Allen*

FARMING

A good farmer is nothing more nor less than a handyman with a sense of humus.
—*E. B. White*

Farming looks mighty easy when your plow is a pencil and you're a thousand miles from the cornfield.
—*Dwight D. Eisenhower*

FAT

I found there was only one way to look thin—hang out with fat people.
—*Rodney Dangerfield*

FATHERS

No man is responsible for his father. That is entirely his mother's affair.
—*Margaret Turnbull*

A boy's best friend is his father, and if he gets up early or stays up late, he may get to see him.

A father is the parent who is busy doing his children's homework while they are busy watching television.

A father is sometimes the master in his own home, but more often merely the paymaster.

When I was fourteen, my father was so ignorant I could hardly stand to have the old man around. When I got to be twenty-one, I was astonished at how much the old man had learned in seven years.
—*Mark Twain*

FATHER'S DAY

Father's Day and Mother's Day are alike, except that on Father's Day you buy a much cheaper gift.

FAULTFINDING

Don't tell your friends their social faults; they will cure the fault and never forgive you.
—*Logan Pearsall Smith*

Fault is one of the easiest things to find, and yet many people keep on looking for it.

Don't criticize your husband's faults. If it weren't for them, he might have married a better wife.

Why can't our neighbors do as we do, and close their eyes to our faults?

FEAR
The man who doesn't know the meaning of the word fear probably doesn't know many other words either.

FEBRUARY FACES
You have such a February face. So full of frost, of storm, and cloudiness.
—*William Shakespeare*

FIFTY
The years between fifty and seventy are the hardest. You are always being asked to do things, and yet you are not decrepit enough to turn them down.
—*T. S. Eliot*

FILING CABINETS
A filing cabinet is a place where you can lose things systematically.
—*T. H. Thompson*

FIRE

He who wishes a fire must put up with the smoke.

FISHERMEN

Old fishermen never die; they just smell that way.

FISHING

Some men in telling a fish story will go to any length.

There is no use in your walking five miles to fish when you can depend on being just as unsuccessful near home.
—*Mark Twain*

FLAPJACKS

There's two sides to every flapjack.

FLATTERY

Nothing is so great an instance of ill manners as flattery. If you flatter all the company, you please none; if you flatter only one or two, you affront the rest.
—*Jonathan Swift*

Everyone likes flattery, and when you come to royalty, you should lay it on with a trowel.
—*Benjamin Disraeli*

Baloney is the unvarnished lie laid on so thick
you hate it. Blarney is flattery laid on so thin you
love it.
—*Bishop Fulton J. Sheen*

FLEAS
Elephants are always drawn smaller than life, but
a flea always larger.
—*Jonathan Swift*

FLIES
Of course, you can catch more flies with honey
than with vinegar, but who needs flies?

FLOODS
The only thing worse than a flooded basement is
a flooded attic.

FLORIDA
It never freezes in Florida, at least not until you've
bought an orange grove.

FLOWERS
Whatever a man's age, he can reduce it several
years by putting a bright-colored flower in his
buttonhole.
—*Mark Twain*

FOG

There's a world of difference between the man who works up steam and the man who generates a fog.

FOLKSINGERS

There are two kinds of folksingers: those who can sing and won't and those who can't sing and do.

FOOLING PEOPLE

You can fool too many of the people too much of the time.
—*James Thurber*

You can fool some of the people all of the time, and all of the people some of the time, but you cannot fool all of the people all the time.
—*Abraham Lincoln*

FOOLPROOF

It is impossible to make anything foolproof because fools are so ingenious.

FOOLS

You can always tell a fool, unless he's hiding inside you.

A fool empties his head every time he opens his mouth.

It is better to keep your mouth shut and be thought a fool than to open it and remove all doubt.
—*Abraham Lincoln*

A fool and his money are soon parted, but seldom by another fool.

If you must be a fool, be one while you're young. It's better to cause grief to parents than to children.

You can only fool some of the people some of the time because the rest of the time they are trying to fool you.

A fool and his money are soon married.
—*Carolyn Wells*

The man who doesn't recognize a fool when he sees one is one himself.
—*Baltasar Gracian*

Never argue with a fool—people might not know the difference.

A man may be a fool and not know it, but not if he is married.
—*H. L. Mencken*

The best blood will sometimes get into a fool or a mosquito.
—*Austin O'Malley*

Fools rush in where bachelors fear to wed.

Wise men talk because they have something to say. Fools talk because they have to say something.
—*Plato*

The world is full of fools, and there's always one more than you think.

If fools went not to market, bad wares would not be sold.
—*John Ray*

FOOTBALL
Football is, after all, a wonderful way to get rid of aggression without going to jail for it.
—*Heywood Hale Broun*

There's only one thing more brutal than a football game, and that's the price of the tickets.

FOOTPRINTS
Some men may not leave footprints on the sands of time, but they certainly leave them everywhere else.

FOREIGN AID
The trouble with foreign aid is that it enables too many countries to live beyond our means.

America's foreign-aid policy is an open book—an open checkbook.

FORGETTING

A mother's advice: I can forget and you can forget, but a piece of paper never forgets.

FORGIVENESS

Women forgive injuries but never forget slights.
—*T. C. Haliburton*

We can forgive most anything except the person who has to forgive us.

Always forgive your enemies—nothing annoys them so much.
—*Oscar Wilde*

Forgive your enemies, but never forget their names.
—*John F. Kennedy*

Forgiveness is the fragrance the violet dashes on the heel that crushes it.

FORTUNE

He who waits upon fortune is never sure of a dinner.
—*Benjamin Franklin*

FOXES

You don't set a fox to watching the chickens just because he has a lot of experience in the hen-house.
—*Harry S. Truman*

Many foxes grow gray but few grow good.
—*Benjamin Franklin*

FRANCE
France has neither winter nor summer nor morals—apart from these drawbacks it is a fine country.
—*Mark Twain*

FRANKNESS
Frank and explicit—that is the right line to take when you wish to conceal your own mind and to confuse the minds of others.
—*Benjamin Disraeli*

FREEDOM
If a man does only what is required of him, he is a slave. The moment he does more, he is a free man.
—*A. W. Robertson*

FREE SPEECH
Why shouldn't speech be free? Very little of it is worth anything.

To say what you think will certainly damage you in society, but a free tongue is worth more than a thousand invitations.
—*Logan Pearsall Smith*

FREE VERSE

Writing free verse is like playing tennis with the net down.
—*Robert Frost*

FRENCH

Maybe the French will get a manned craft into space if they can get a rocket strong enough to lift a bottle of wine.
—*David Brinkley*

FRICTION

Change means movement, movement means friction, friction means heat, and heat means controversy. The only place where there is no friction is in outer space or a seminar on political action.
—*Saul Alinsky*

FRIENDS

You can always tell a real friend: When you've made a fool of yourself, he doesn't feel you've done a permanent job.

A true friend laughs at your stories even when they're not so good and sympathizes with your troubles even when they're not so bad.

To accept a favor from a friend is to confer one.
—*John Churton Collins*

Anyone can sympathize with the sufferings of a friend, but it requires a very fine nature to sympathize with a friend's success.
—*Oscar Wilde*

Your friend is the man who knows all about you and still likes you.
—*Elbert Hubbard*

To find a friend one must close one eye; to keep him, two.
—*Norman Douglas*

He who is his own friend is a friend to all men.
—*Seneca*

If a friend is in trouble, don't annoy him by asking if there is anything you can do. Think up something appropriate and do it.
—*Ed How*

A real friend is one who walks in when the rest of the world walks out.
—*Walter Winchell*

You can't eat your friends and have them too.
—*Budd Schulberg*

If all men knew what each said of the other, there would not be four friends in the world.
—*Blaise Pascal*

FRIENDSHIP

Friendship is like money, easier made than kept.
—*Samuel Butler*

Friendship, like gold, needs the acid test of adversity to determine its value.

The best way to keep friendships from breaking is not to drop them.

FROWNING

Keep frowning; some people may give you credit for thinking.

FUN

There is no fun in having nothing to do; the fun is in having lots to do and not doing it.

There ain't much fun in medicine, but there's a good deal of medicine in fun.
—*Josh Billings*

FUNERAL

Why is it that we rejoice at a birth and grieve at a funeral? It is because we are not the person involved.
—*Mark Twain*

I did not attend his funeral, but I wrote a nice letter saying I approved it.
—*Mark Twain*

The reason so many people turned up at his funeral is that they wanted to make sure he was dead.

FUNNY

You can teach taste and editorial sense, but the ability to say something funny is something I've never been able to teach anyone.
—*Abe Burrows*

Some fellers' idea o' being funny is breakin' a few bones when they shake your hand.
—*Frank McKinney Hubbard*

FUNNY BONE

The man and woman who can laugh at their love, who can kiss with smiles and embrace with chuckles, will outlast in mutual affection all the throat-lumpy, cow-eyed couples of their acquaintance. Nothing lives on so fresh and evergreen as the love with a funny bone.

You see, dear, it is not true that woman was made from man's rib; she was really made from his funny bone.
—*James M. Barrie*

FUR COATS

Most fur coats come from the male animal.

FURNITURE

I used to sell furniture for a living. The trouble
was it was my own.
—*Les Dawson*

FUTURE

The trouble with our times is that the future is not
what it used to be.
—*Paul Valery*

The future is never made any brighter by burning
the candle at both ends.

GAMBLING
As long as a man follows the races, he is bound to be behind.

GAP
There was a gap between what went on in his mind and what came out of his mouth.
—*James M. Cain*

GARAGES
If your garage is too small, you can always enlarge it by having your wife park your car.

GARBAGE
During the garbage strike here's how I got rid of my garbage: I gift wrapped it, left it in my car, and they stole it.
—*Henny Youngman*

GARDENERS
Nothing discourages an amateur gardener like watch- ing his family eat the entire garden at one meal.

Old gardeners never die; they just spade away.

GARDENING
The chief objection to gardening is that by the time your back gets used to it, your enthusiasm is gone.

I've had enough of gardening—I'm just about ready to throw in the trowel.

GARDEN OF EDEN

It wasn't an apple from the tree that started the trouble in the Garden of Eden; it was the pair on the ground.

GARDENS

I had great luck with my garden this year—nothing came up.

A garden is a thing of beauty and a job forever.

People who think they can run the earth should begin with a small garden.

GENIUS

Genius is one percent inspiration and 99 percent perspiration.
—*Thomas A. Edison*

Genius, in one respect, is like gold—numbers of persons are constantly writing about both, who have neither.
—*C. C. Colton*

The mark of talent is to do the possible with ease; the mark of genius is to do the impossible with difficulty.

Nothing spoils a good party like a genius.
—*Elsa Maxwell*

Thousands of geniuses live and die undiscovered— either by themselves or by others.
—*Mark Twain*

GENTLEMEN

A gentleman is one who never hurts anyone's feelings unintentionally.
—*Oliver Herford*

A gentleman is a man who has trained himself to yawn in such a way that you think he is smiling at you.

The man who is always talking about being a gentleman never is one.
—*Robert S. Surtees*

To be born a gentleman is an accident; to die a gentleman is an achievement.

A gentleman is a man who can play the accordion but doesn't.

GENTLENESS

The one human characteristic that can make a person stand out above all others in a group is a mannerism of complete gentleness.

GIVING

From what we get, we can make a living; what we give, however, makes a life.
—*Arthur Ashe*

GOALS

Whenever you have an aim, you must sacrifice something of freedom to attain it.
—*Somerset Maugham*

GOD

God is not a cosmic bellboy for whom we can press a button to get things.
—*Harry Emerson Fosdick*

Nobody talks so constantly about God as those who insist that there is no God.
—*Heywood Broun*

God created man in his own image, says the Bible, and the philosophers do just the opposite—they create God in theirs.
—*George Lichtenberg*

Some people want an affidavit from God that he really exists.
—*Danny Thomas*

If God is dead, who will save the queen?

I am not concerned whether God is on my side or not, but I am concerned whether I am on God's side.
—*Abraham Lincoln*

You need not tell a child that there is a God.

Many people deny that there is a God, our God, or the concept of God. But I have never met anybody who did not want there to be a God.
—*Viktor E. Frankl*

What can you say about a society that says God is dead and Elvis is alive?
—*Irv Kupcinet*

GOING OUT ON A LIMB
Why not go out on a limb? Isn't that where the fruit is?
—*Frank Scully*

GOLF
The only way a minister can meet his flock is to join a golf club.

If you watch a game, it's fun; if you play it, it's recreation; if you work at it, it's golf.

Golf develops a beginner's self-control, but caddying for a beginner develops it even more.

The greatest disappointment in a golfer's life is when he makes a hole-in-one without witnesses.

GOOD
The word good has many meanings. For example, if a man were to shoot his grandmother at a range of five hundred yards, I should call him a good shot but not necessarily a good man.
—*G. K. Chesterton*

To be good is noble, but to teach others how to be good is nobler—and less trouble.
—*Mark Twain*

GOOD ACTIONS
The greatest pleasure I know is to do a good action by stealth and to have it found out by accident.
—*Charles Lamb*

GOOD BREEDING
Good breeding consists in concealing how much we think of ourselves and how little we think of the other person.
—*Mark Twain*

GOOD EXAMPLES

Few things are harder to put up with than the annoyance of a good example.
—*Mark Twain*

GOOD FORTUNE

A man is never so on trial as in the moment of excessive good fortune.
—*Lew Wallace*

GOOD LOSERS

Everyone likes a good loser, especially if he's on the other side.

GOODNESS

There are bad people who would be less dangerous if they were quite devoid of goodness.
—*François La Rochefoucauld*

GOOD OLD DAYS

If you're yearning for the good old days, just turn off the air-conditioning.
—*Griff Niblack*

The good old days! I won't say I'm out of condition now—but I even puff going downstairs.
—*Dick Gregory*

Nothing is more responsible for the good old days than a bad memory.
—*Franklin P. Adams*

GOSSIP

Gossip is the only sound that travels faster than sound.

The difference between news and gossip lies in whether you raise your voice or lower it.
—*Franklin P. Jones*

If you haven't got anything nice to say about anybody, come sit next to me.
—*Alice Roosevelt Longworth*

There isn't much to be seen in a little town, but what you hear makes up for it.
—*Frank McKinney Hubbard*

The only time people dislike gossip is when you gossip about them.
—*Will Rogers*

Blessed are the hard of hearing for they shall miss much idle gossip.

Girl: "Of course I wouldn't say anything about her unless I could say something good. And, oh boy, is this good!"
—*Bill King*

Usually when the woman who is talking lowers her voice, the woman who is listening raises her eyebrows.

The difference between gossip and news depends on whether you are telling it or hearing it.

A gossip's idea of generosity is to keep nothing to himself.

GOVERNMENT

It's getting harder and harder to support the government in the style to which it has become accustomed.

I don't make jokes; I just watch the government and report the facts.
—*Will Rogers*

Government is like a baby—an alimentary canal with a big appetite at one end and no sense of responsibility at the other.
—*Ronald Reagan*

One of the things we have to be thankful for is that we don't get as much government as we pay for.
—*Charles F. Kettering*

I don't know what people have got against the government; they've done nothing.
—*Bob Hope*

The government is the only known vessel that leaks from the top.
—*James Reston*

You cannot get blood from a stone, but you can get a government grant to try.
—*Louis Phillips*

The nine most terrifying words in the English language are "I'm from the government, and I'm here to help."

GOVERNMENT GRANTS

Those who can't teach, teach the teachers. Those who can't teach the teachers get government grants.

GRAPEFRUIT

A: There's a lot of juice in this grapefruit.

B: Yes—more than meets the eye!

GRAVITY

It's a good thing there's gravity or else when birds die, they'd stay where they were.
—*Steven Wright*

GREATNESS

Some are born great, some achieve greatness, and others thrust greatness upon themselves.

Some are born great, some achieve greatness, and others just grate.

GRIEF
Everyone can master a grief but he that has it.
—*William Shakespeare*

GROCERS
Grocers do not groce.

GROSS IGNORANCE
Gross ignorance: 144 times worse than ordinary ignorance.
—*Bennett Cerf*

GROWING OLDER
You are not permitted to kill a woman who has injured you, but nothing forbids you to reflect that she is growing older every minute. You are avenged 1,440 times a day.
—*Ambrose Bierce*

GUESTS
The art of being a good guest is to know when to leave.
—*Prince Philip*

Some guests spend most of the evening between the time they get up to say good-bye and the time they leave.

There are two kinds of guests: those who come after dinner and those who come after dinner.

GUINEA PIGS

Guinea pigs are not pigs, nor do they come from Guinea.

HABIT

Habit is habit and not to be flung out of the window by any man, but coaxed downstairs a step at a time.
—*Mark Twain*

The chains of habit are too weak to be felt until they are too strong to be broken.
—*Samuel Johnson*

HABITS

Nothing so needs reforming as other people's habits.
—*Mark Twain*

The second half of a man's life is made up of nothing but the habits acquired during the first half.
—*Fyodor Dostoevski*

HALO

A halo has to fall only a few inches to become a noose.

HANDSOME

Twenty-four years ago, madam, I was incredibly handsome. The remains of it are still visible through the rift of time. I was so handsome that women became spellbound when I came in view. In San Francisco, in rainy seasons, I was frequently mistaken for a cloudless day.
—*Mark Twain*

HANDWRITING ON THE WALL

When a man sees the handwriting on the wall,
there's probably a child in the family.

HAPPINESS

It's pretty hard to tell what does bring happiness.
Poverty an' wealth have both failed.
—*Frank McKinney Hubbard*

Happiness is a way station between too little and
too much.
—*Channing Pollock*

Gather the crumbs of happiness, and you will have
a loaf of contentment.

Real happiness don't consist so much in what a
man don't have as it does in what he don't want.
—*Josh Billings*

Happiness is no laughing matter.
—*Richard Whately*

Happiness is a habit.
—*Elbert Hubbard*

Most folks are about as happy as they make up
their minds to be.
—*Abraham Lincoln*

If you would make a man happy, do not add to his
possessions but subtract from his desires.
—*Seneca*

HAPPY MOMENTS

Cherish all your happy moments; they make a fine cushion for old age.
—*Booth Tarkington*

HARD WORK

When a man tells you that he got rich through hard work, ask him, "Whose?"
—*Don Marqui*

Hard work never killed anybody, but why take a chance?

Hard work never killed anybody, but it sure has scared a lot of folks to death.

HARVARD

You can always tell a Harvard man, but you cannot tell him much.

HATCHETS

Do not use a hatchet to remove a fly from your friend's forehead.

HATRED

The man has no occasion to hate me—I can't recall that I ever did him a favor.
—*Benjamin Disraeli*

Hating people is like burning down your own house to get rid of a rat.
—*Harry Emerson Fosdick*

HATS

A candidate needs four hats: one to cover his head, another to throw into the ring, a third to pass around, and finally one to talk through.

HEADLIGHTS

The faults of others are like headlights of an approaching car—they always seem more glaring than our own.

HEALTH

The only way to keep your health is to eat what you don't want, drink what you don't like, and do what you'd rather not. The average heart specialist can usually check the condition of his patient's heart simply by sending him a bill.
—*Mark Twain*

Quit worrying about your health. It'll go away.
—*Robert Orben*

Nothing gives his friends more pleasure than when a health faddist becomes ill.

HEARSES

The driver of a hearse has the advantage of never having to put up with backseat driving.
—*Douglas Yates*

HEART

Words that come from the heart enter the heart.

Trust your heart. . . . Never deny it a hearing. It is the kind of house oracle that often foretells the most important.
—*Balthasar Gracian*

HEARTBURN

No country can touch us when it comes to heartburn and upset stomachs. This nation, under God, with liberty and justice for all, neutralizes more stomach acid in one day than the Soviet Union does in a year. We give more relief from discomfort of the intestinal tract than China and Japan combined.

HEAT

If you don't like the heat, get out of the kitchen.
—*Harry S. Truman*

HELL

The hottest places in hell are reserved for those who in a time of great moral crisis maintain their neutrality.
—*Dante*

There have been many definitions of hell, but for the English the best definition is that it is a place where the Germans are the police, the Swedish are the comedians, the Italians are the defense force, Frenchmen dig the roads, the Belgians are the pop singers, the Spanish run the railways, the Turks cook the food, the Irish are the waiters, the Greeks run the government, and the common language is Dutch.
—*David Frost*

I never give them hell. I just tell the truth, and they think it's hell.
—*Harry S. Truman*

HELPING HAND

The man who is looking for a helping hand can always find one attached to his arm.

HEROES

We can't all be heroes, because somebody has to sit on the curb and clap as they go by.
—*Will Rogers*

HESITATION

He who hesitates is not only lost but several miles from the next freeway exit.

HIGH HEELS

High heels—invented by a woman who had been kissed on the forehead.
—*Christopher Morley*

HIGHEST PRICE

The highest price we can pay for anything is to ask it.
—*W. S. Landor*

HIGHLIGHTS

The highlight of my childhood was making my brother laugh so hard that food came out of his nose.
—*Garrison Keillor*

HIGHWAYS

Three-quarters of our population live in or near cities; the other quarter is on the highway looking for the exit.

HINDSIGHT

If the hindsight of some women was as good as their foresight, they wouldn't be wearing slacks.

If a man had half as much foresight as he has twice as much hindsight, he'd be a lot better off.
—*Robert J. Burdette*

HISTORIANS
Very few things happen at the right time, and the rest do not happen at all. The conscientious historian will correct these defects.
—*Herodotus*

HISTORY
History is simply a piece of paper covered with print; the main thing is still to make history, not to write it.
—*Otto von Bismarck*

HOLIDAYS
Holidays are often overrated disturbances of routine, costly and uncomfortable; and they usually need another holiday to correct their ravages.
—*Edward Verrall Lucas*

HOLLYWOOD
Hollywood is a city in the U.S. where someone is more likely to ask you who's whose than who's who.

You can take all the sincerity in Hollywood, place it in the navel of a fruit fly, and still have room enough for three caraway seeds and a producer's heart.
—*Fred Allen*

Behind the phony tinsel of Hollywood lies the real tinsel.
—*Oscar Levant*

As I was going to St. Ives
I met a man with seven wives,
So I figured I was pretty near Hollywood.
—*Jack Sharkey*

HOME
Home is where you go when you're tired of being polite to people.

HONESTY
There's one way to find out if a man is honest: Ask him. If he says yes, you know he is crooked.
—*Mark Twain / Groucho Marx*

Honesty is the best policy
. . . but not the cheapest.
. . . when there is money in it.
. . . most of the time.
. . . there's less competition.
—*Mark Twain*

HORSEBACK
There's nothing like your first horseback ride to make you feel better off.

HORSES
I'd horsewhip you if I had a horse.
—*Groucho Marx*

I did not say this meat was tough. I just said I didn't see the horse that usually stands outside.
—*W. C. Fields*

HOT MEALS
The last time I had a hot meal was when a candle fell in my TV dinner.

HOT WATER
If you find yourself in hot water, take a bath.
—*Henny Youngman*

The teakettle is up to its neck in hot water but sings a merry tune.

HOUSEWORK
I hate housework! You make the beds, you do the dishes—and six months later you have to start all over again.
—*Joan Rivers*

HUMANNESS

To err is human; to blame it on someone else is even more human.

The full potentialities of human fury cannot be reached until a friend of both parties tactfully intervenes.
—*G. K. Chesterton*

HUMBLE PIE

If humble pie has to be eaten, that's the best way to eat it—bolt it whole.
—*Maurice Hewlett*

HUMOR

Humor is when the joke is on you but hits the other fellow first—before it boomerangs.
—*Langston Hughes*

A man without mirth is like a wagon without springs. He is jolted disagreeably by every pebble in the road.
—*Henry Ward Beecher*

Lord, give me a sense of humor that I may take some happiness from this life and share it with others.
—*Thomas Moore*

When you've killed the sense of humor of a nation, you've killed the nation.
—*Red Skelton*

One doesn't have a sense of humor. It has you.
—*Larry Gelbart*

Analyzing humor is like dissecting a frog: Few people are interested, and the frog dies.
—*E. B. White*

There seems to be no limits to which humorless people will not go to analyze humor. It seems to worry them. They can't believe that anything could be so funny just on its own hook.
—*Robert Benchley*

Good humor is the suspenders that keep our working clothes on.

Humor is emotional chaos remembered in tranquility.
—*James Thurber*

Mark my words, when a society has to resort to the lavatory for its humor, the writing is on the wall.
—*Alan Bennett*

HUMORISTS

Think of what would happen to us in America if there were no humorists; life would be one long *Congressional Record.*
—*Thomas L. Masson*

HUSBANDS

Being a husband is like any other job—it helps if you like the boss.

Half a loafer is better than no husband at all.
—*Louis Safian*

A husband's job is to keep talking to unexpected guests at the front gate while his wife straightens out the living room.

HUSTLES

Everything comes to him who hustles while he waits.
—*Thomas A. Edison*

HYPOCHONDRIACS

A hypochondriac never gets cured of any disease until he acquires another.

A hypochondriac is one who has a pill for everything except what ails him.

IDEALISTS

An idealist is one who, on noticing that a rose smells better than a cabbage, concludes that it will also make better soup.
—*H. L. Mencken*

IDEAL WIVES

An ideal wife is any woman who has an ideal husband.
—*Booth Tarkington*

IDEAL WOMAN

The ideal woman . . . the dream of a man who will be a bachelor all his life.
—*W. Burton Baldry*

IDEAS

There is no defense, except stupidity, against the impact of a new idea.
—*P. W. Bridgman*

I had a monumental idea this morning, but I didn't like it.
—*Sam Goldwyn*

Ideas are like children: There are none so wonderful as your own.

I am long on ideas but short on time.

IDLE WORDS

As we must account for every idle word, so we must for every idle silence.
—*Benjamin Franklin*

IGNORANCE

If ignorance is bliss, why aren't there more happy people?

You can't underestimate the ignorance of some people.

Every now and then you meet a man whose ignorance is encyclopedic.
—*Stanislaw J. Lec*

What you don't know would make a great book.
—*Sydney Smith*

What he doesn't know would make a library anybody would be proud of.

He was distinguished for ignorance, for he had only one idea, and that was wrong.
—*Benjamin Disraeli*

There is only one thing more widely distributed than experience, and that is ignorance.

When ignorance gets started, it knows no bounds.
—*Will Rogers*

Never try to tell everything you know. It may take too short a time.
—*Norman Ford*

All you need in this life is ignorance and confidence; then success is sure.
—*Mark Twain*

I'm still waiting for some college to come up with a march protesting student ignorance.
—*Paul Larmer*

It is impossible to defeat an ignorant man in argument.
—*William G. McAdoo*

IGNORE

I don't pay any attention to him. I don't even ignore him.
—*Sam Goldwyn*

IMAGINATION

His imagination resembled the wings of an ostrich. It enabled him to run, though not to soar.
—*Thomas Babington Macaulay*

IMBALANCED

One out of four people in this country is mentally imbalanced. Think of your three closest friends— if they seem okay, then you're the one.
—*Ann Landers*

IMITATION

When people are free to do as they please, they usually imitate each other.
—*Eric Hoffer*

IMPATIENCE

The man who hasn't time to stop at a railroad crossing always finds time to attend the funeral.

IMPOSSIBLE

Blessed are they who have learned to accept the impossible, do without the indispensable, and bear the intolerable.

IMPROMPTU SPEECHES

It usually takes me more than three weeks to prepare a good impromptu speech.
—*Mark Twain*

IN AND OUT

A woman shopping in a department store noticed that the clerk behind the complaint desk smiled at everyone who talked to her and kept her voice low and pleasant, even when irate customers spoke rudely to her. The shopper was amazed at the way the woman kept her cool. Then she noticed the clerk's dark earrings. On one, in white lettering, was inscribed "In," and on the other, "Out."

INANIMATE OBJECTS

Inanimate objects can be classified scientifically into three major categories: those that don't work, those that break down, and those that get lost.
—*Russell Baker*

INCOME

The two most important things about your income are: Make it first, and then make it last.

INCOME TAX

Income tax returns are the most imaginative fiction being written today.

The income tax is a neat plan devised to clean you out of your filthy lucre.

Income tax has made more liars out of the American people than golf.
—*Will Rogers*

INCOMPETENCE

If at first you don't succeed, you may be at your level of incompetence already.
—*Laurence J. Peter*

INDECISION

His indecision is final.

INDEPENDENCE
Some husbands assert their independence by refusing to wear an apron while doing the dishes.

INDIFFERENCE
Nothing is so fatal to religion as indifference, which is, at least, half infidelity.
—*Edmund Burke*

I don't care about that; it rolls off my back like a duck.
—*Samuel Goldwyn*

INDISPENSABLE
The graveyards are full of indispensable men.
—*Charles de Gaulle*

If you feel that you are indispensable, put your finger in a glass of water, withdraw it, and note the hole you have left.

INFLATION
Invest in inflation. It's the only thing going up.
—*Will Rogers*

Inflation has created a new economic problem: windfall poverty.

A little inflation is like a little pregnancy—it keeps on growing.
—*Leon Henderson*

INHERITANCE

Never say you know another entirely until you have divided an inheritance with him.
—*Johann Kaspar Lavater*

INSANITY

In things pertaining to enthusiasm, no man is sane who does not know how to be insane on proper occasions.
—*Henry Ward Beecher*

Insanity is hereditary—you get it from your children.
—*Sam Levenson*

INSECTS

When the insects take over the world, we hope they will remember with gratitude how we took them along on all our picnics.
—*Bill Vaughan*

INSOLENCE

Prosperity is the surest breeder of insolence I know.
—*Mark Twain*

INSOMNIA

Insomnia: a contagious disease transmitted from babies to parents.

His insomnia was so bad he couldn't sleep even during office hours.
—*Arthur Baer*

INSPIRING
He is useless on top of the ground; he ought to be under it, inspiring the cabbages.
—*Mark Twain*

INSUFFERABLE
When a man is young, he is so wild he is insufferable. When he is old, he plays the saint and becomes insufferable again.
—*Nikolai Gogol*

INTELLIGENCE
An intelligence test sometimes shows a man how smart he would have been not to have taken it.
—*Laurence J. Peter*

INTELLIGENT LIFE
Sometimes I think the surest sign that intelligent life exists elsewhere in the universe is that none of it has tried to contact us.
—*Bill Watterson*

INTENTIONS
The hardest task in a girl's life is to prove to a man that his intentions are serious.
—Helen Rowland

INTUITION
Intuition: that strange instinct that tells a woman she is right, whether she is or not.

IQ
When your IQ rises to 28, sell.
—Professor Irwin Corey

IRONS IN THE FIRE
The man who has too many irons in the fire usually gets his fingers burned.

IRRITATING
There is nobody so irritating as somebody with less intelligence and more sense than we have.
—Don Herold

IRS
The three Rs of the Internal Revenue Service: This is ours; that is ours; everything is ours.

Whoever said you can't take it with you must have been an IRS agent.

JAYWALKING

For that tired, run-down feeling, try jaywalking.

JEALOUSY

Love may be blind, but jealousy sees too much.

JEWELRY

Jewelry takes people's minds off your wrinkles.
—*Sonja Henie*

JIGSAW

They call him "Jigsaw" because every time he's faced with a problem, he goes to pieces.

JOBS

It's a recession when your neighbor loses his job; it's a depression when you lose yours.
—*Harry S. Truman*

The feeling that you've done a job well is rewarding; the feeling that you've done it perfectly is fatal.

The ugliest of trades have their moments of enjoyment. If I were a gravedigger, or even a hangman, there are some people I could work for with a good deal of enjoyment.
—*Douglas Jerrold*

JOKES

For every ten jokes, thou has got an hundred
enemies.
—*Laurence Sterne*

JOURNALISM

Literature is the art of writing something that will
be read twice; journalism what will be read once.
—*Cyril Connolly*

JOURNALISTS

Journalists say a thing that they know isn't true
in the hope that if they keep on saying it long
enough it will be true.
—*Arnold Bennett*

JOY

Grief can take care of itself, but to get the full
value of a joy you must have somebody to divide it
with.
—*Mark Twain*

JUDAS

Still as of old, men by themselves are priced—
For thirty pieces Judas sold himself, not Christ.
—*Hester H. Cholmodeley*

JUDGMENT

The man who is forever criticizing his wife's judgment never seems to question her choice of a husband.

JUDO

The Japanese have a word for it. It's judo—the art of conquering by yielding. The Western equivalent of judo is "Yes, dear."
—*J. P. McEvoy*

JUMPING TO CONCLUSIONS

I am no athlete, but at one sport I used to be an expert. It was a dangerous game called "jumping to conclusions."
—*Eddie Cantor*

JURY DUTY

When you go into court, you are putting your fate into the hands of twelve people who weren't smart enough to get out of jury duty.
—*Norm Crosby*

The jury system puts a ban upon intelligence and honesty and a premium upon ignorance, stupidity, and perjury.
—*Mark Twain*

We have a criminal jury system which is superior to any in the world; and its efficiency is only marred by the difficulty of finding twelve men every day who don't know anything and can't read.
—*Mark Twain*

KEEPING UP WITH THE JONESES

Never keep up with the Joneses. Drag them down to your level—it's cheaper.
—*Quentin Crisp*

About the time you catch up with the Joneses, they start to refinance.

KEEPING YOUR HEAD

If you can keep your head when all about you are losing theirs, it's just possible you haven't grasped the situation.
—*Jean Kerr*

KEEPING YOUR MOUTH SHUT

An open mouth has a tendency to invite a foot.

Keep your mouth shut, and you will never put your foot in it.

Breathe through your nose—it keeps the mouth shut.

It is better to keep your mouth shut and appear stupid than to open it and remove all doubt.
—*Mark Twain*

As you go through life, you are going to have many opportunities to keep your mouth shut. Take advantage of all of them.

KIDS

I've seen kids ride bicycles, run, play ball, set up a camp, swing, fight a war, swim, and race for eight hours . . . yet have to be driven to the garbage can.
—*Erma Bombeck*

When I was a kid, my parents moved a lot—but I always found them.
—*Rodney Dangerfield*

KINDERGARTEN

Children start kindergarten these days with a big advantage: They already know two letters of the alphabet—TV.

KINDNESS

One of the most difficult things to give away is kindness—it is usually returned.

KINDS OF PEOPLE

There will always be two kinds of people: those who say what they think, and those who keep their friends.

There are four types of men in this world:
The man who knows and knows that he knows; he is
wise, so consult him.
The man who knows but doesn't know that he knows;
help him not forget what he knows.
The man who knows not and knows that he knows not;
teach him.
Finally, there is the man who knows not but pretends
that he knows; he is a fool, so avoid him.
—Solomon Ibn Gabirol

KISSES
The sound of a kiss is not so loud as that of a cannon, but its echo lasts a great deal longer.
—Oliver Wendell Holmes

KITCHEN SINK
Before marriage he promised her everything but the kitchen sink; after marriage the kitchen sink was all she got.
—Richard Needham

KLEPTOMANIA
Kleptomaniac: a person who helps himself because he can't help himself.
—Henry Morgan

KNAVES

Who friendship with a knave has made
Is judged a partner in the trade.
—John Gay

KNOWLEDGE

Strange how much you've got to know before you know how little you know.

Knowledge rests not upon truth alone but upon error also.
—C. G. Jung

Since we cannot know all that is to be known of anything, we ought to know a little about everything.
—Blaise Pascal

The less you know about a subject, the longer it takes you to explain it.

Universities are full of knowledge: The freshmen bring a little in, and the seniors take none away, so knowledge accumulates.
—Abbott Lawrence Lowell

LABOR DAY

If all the cars in the United States were placed end to end, it would probably be Labor Day weekend.
—*Doug Larson*

LACK OF HUMOR

Men will confess to treason, murder, arson, false teeth, or a wig. How many of them will own up to a lack of humor?
—*Frank Moore Colby*

LANGUAGE

Drawing on my fine command of language, I said nothing.
—*Robert Benchley*

LATENESS

I have noticed that the people who are late are often so much jollier than the people who have to wait for them.
—*E. V. Lucas*

LAUGHTER

If you're not allowed to laugh in heaven, I don't want to go there.
—*Martin Luther*

He who laughs last just got the joke.

Laughter is not a bad beginning for a friendship, and it is the best ending for one.
—*Oscar Wilde*

Laughter is the sensation of feeling good all over and showing it principally in one spot.
—*Josh Billings*

Strange, when you come to think of it, that of all the countless folk who have lived before our time on this planet not one is known in history or in legend as having died of laughter.
—*Max Beerbohm*

LAW
We are in bondage to the law in order that we may be free.
—*Cicero*

LAWYERS
A lawyer will do anything to win a case. Sometimes he will even tell the truth.
—*Patrick Murray*

Ignorance of the law does not prevent the losing lawyer from collecting his bill.

Personally, I don't think you can make a lawyer honest by an act of legislature. You've got to work on his conscience. And his lack of conscience is what makes him a lawyer.
—*Will Rogers*

A lawyer is a learned gentleman who rescues your estate from your enemies and keeps it for himself.
—*Lord Brougham*

Here's an amazing story: A man in Orlando, Florida, was hit by eight cars in a row, and only one stopped. The first seven drivers thought he was a lawyer. The eighth was a lawyer.
—*Jay Leno*

Why is it that when you need a lawyer, you can always find one?

Talk is cheap . . . except when you hire a lawyer.
—*Joey Adams*

If the thing a man wants to do is right, he goes ahead and does it. If it is wrong, he consults an attorney.

If God helped those who help themselves, those who help themselves wouldn't have to hire expensive lawyers.
—*Leo Rosten*

The first thing we do, let's kill all the lawyers.
—*William Shakespeare*

If a man dies and leaves his estate in an uncertain condition, the lawyers become his heirs.
—*Ed Howe*

Last winter it was so cold that lawyers walked around with their hands in their own pockets.

There are three reasons why lawyers are replacing rats as laboratory research animals: One is that they are plentiful, another is that the lab assistants don't get so attached to them, and the third is that they will do things you just can't get rats to do.
—*Blanche Knott*

I wanted to make it a law that only those lawyers and attorneys should receive fees who had won their cases. How much litigation would have been prevented by such a measure!
—*Napoléon Bonaparte*

LEADERSHIP

Lead, follow, or get out of the way.

If two ride on a horse, one must ride behind.
—*William Shakespeare*

I must follow them. I am their leader.
—*Andrew Bonar*

There are two kinds of leaders in the world—some are interested in the fleeces, others in the flock.

When you are getting kicked from the rear, it means you're in front.
—*Bishop Fulton J. Sheen*

The person who knows how will always have a job. But the person who knows why will be boss.
—*Carl Wood*

LEARNING

A little learning is a dangerous thing, but at college it is the usual thing.

The important thing is not so much that every child should be taught as that every child should be given the wish to learn.
—*John Lubbock*

Learning is not child's play; we cannot learn without pain.
—*Aristotle*

Swallow all your learning in the morning, but digest it in company in the evenings.
—*Lord Chesterfield*

LEGISLATURES

Never blame a legislative body for not doing something. When they do nothing, that don't hurt anybody. When they do something is when they become dangerous.
—*Will Rogers*

LEISURE

Leisure is the two minutes' rest a man gets while his wife is thinking up something else for him to do.

LENDING BOOKS

Never lend books, for no one ever returns them;
the only books I have in my library are books that
other folk have lent me.
—*Anatole France*

The definition of a rare volume is a returned
book.

LESSONS

It seems like one o' the hardest lessons t' be
learned in this life is where your business ends an'
somebody else's begins.

LEVITY

A little levity will save many a good heavy thing
from sinking.
—*Samuel Butler*

LIARS

Even a liar tells a hundred truths to one lie; he has
to, to make the lie good for anything.
—*Henry Ward Beecher*

LIBERALS

A liberal mind is a mind that is able to imagine
itself believing anything.
—*Max Eastman*

A liberal is a person whose interests aren't at stake at the moment.
—*Willis Player*

A liberal is a man who is willing to spend somebody else's money.
—*Senator Carter Glass*

A liberal is a man who leaves the room when the fight begins.
—*Heywood Broun*

As usual the Liberals offer a mixture of sound and original ideas. Unfortunately, none of the sound ideas is original and none of the original ideas is sound.
—*Harold Macmillan*

LIBERTY
Liberty means responsibility. That is why most men dread it.
—*George Bernard Shaw*

LIES
One of the most striking differences between a cat and a lie is that a cat has only nine lives.
—*Mark Twain*

A lie always needs a truth for a handle to it. The worst lies are those whose blade is false but whose handle is true.
—*Henry Ward Beecher*

You can't tell—maybe a fish goes home and lies about the size of the man he got away from.

Those who feel it is okay to tell white lies soon go color-blind.

LIFE

Almost everything in life is easier to get into than out of.

Life cannot wait until the sciences may have explained the universe scientifically. We cannot put off living until we are ready. The most salient characteristic of life is its coerciveness: It is always urgent, "here and now," without any possible postponement. Life is fired at us point-blank.

If there is a sin against life, it consists perhaps not so much in despairing of life as in hoping for another life and in eluding the implacable grandeur of this life.
—*Albert Camus*

The best things in life aren't things.
—*Art Buchwald*

Life must be understood backwards. But . . . it must be lived forward.
—*Søren Kierkegaard*

Life is what happens to you while you're making other plans.
—*Robert Balzer*

Life is like a shower: One false move, and you're in hot water.

Life begins when the kids leave home and the dog dies.

Life is like a taxi ride: The meter keeps on ticking whether you're getting anywhere or not.

Life is something to do when you can't get to sleep.
—*Fran Lebowitz*

The first forty years of life give us the text, the next thirty the commentary.
—*Arthur Schopenhauer*

Life is made up of sobs, sniffles, and smiles, with sniffles predominating.
—*O. Henry*

When life hands you a lemon, make lemonade.

Live each day as if it were your last . . . and some-day you will be right.
—*Thomas Ken*

LIPS
If your lips you would keep from slips,
Five things observe with care:
Of whom you speak, to whom you speak,
And how and when and where.

Once a word has left one's lips, even a team of four horses cannot overtake it.

LITERATURE
Literature is a very bad crutch but a very good walking stick.
—*Charles Lamb*

LONESOMENESS
Every time I look at you I get a fierce desire to be lonesome.
—*Oscar Levant*

LONG STORIES
To make a long story short, there's nothing like having the boss walk in.
—*Doris Lilly*

When a fellow says, "Well, to make a long story short," it's too late.
—*Don Herold*

LOOKING BACK
If you look back too much, you will soon be heading that way.

LOOKS
He gave her a look you could've poured on a waffle.
—*Ring Lardner*

She looked, as far as her clothes went, as though
she had been pulled through brambles and then
pushed through a thin tube.
—*Gwyn Thomas*

LOS ANGELES

The difference between Los Angeles and yogurt is
that yogurt has real culture.
—*Tom Taussik*

LOVE

No woman ever hates a man for being in love with
her, but many a woman hates a man for being a
friend to her.
—*Alexander Pope*

Love is an ocean of emotions surrounded by
expenses.
—*Lord Dewar*

Love blinds us to faults, but hatred blinds us to
virtues.
—*Ibn Ezra*

If Jack's in love, he's no judge of Jill's beauty.
—*Benjamin Franklin*

Love may be blind, but it certainly finds its way
around in the dark.

Love is like the measles: We all have to go through it.

Love and a cough cannot be hid.
—*George Herbert*

Life is just one foolish thing after another, and love is just two foolish things after each other.

Some people are born silly, some acquire silliness, and others fall in love.

Love is the only fire against which there is no insurance.

When in love try not to say foolish things; if you succeed, you are not in love.

Love is that funny feeling you feel when you feel that you have a feeling you have never felt before.

Love is like the measles: We can have it but once, and the later in life we have it, the tougher it goes with us.
—*Josh Billings*

Love often makes a fool of the cleverest men and as often gives cleverness to the most foolish.

Love cures people—both the ones who give it and the ones who receive it.
—*Dr. Karl Menninger*

Love is an obsessive delusion that is cured by marriage.
—*Dr. Karl Bowman*

LUCID

Ordinarily he is insane, but he has lucid moments when he is only stupid.
—*Heinrich Heine*

LUGGAGE

The scientific theory I like best is that the rings of Saturn are composed entirely of lost airline luggage.
—*Mark Russell*

LYING

Lying is like trying to hide in a fog: If you move about you're in danger of bumping your head against the truth, and as soon as the fog blows off, you are gone anyhow.
—*Josh Billings*

MAJOR PROBLEMS

My wife and I made a bargain many years ago that in order to live harmoniously, I would decide all the major problems and she would decide all the unimportant problems. So far, in our twenty-five years of matrimony, we have never had any major problems.
—*Judge Jonah Goldstein*

MAKING A LIVING

The world would be a pleasant place if there weren't so many fools in it, but it would be harder to make a living.

MAKING THINGS HAPPEN

Some people make things happen, some watch things happen, while others wonder what has happened.

MAN

We need not worry so much about what man descends from—it's what he descends to that shames the human race.
—*Mark Twain*

Man is certainly stark mad. He cannot make a worm, and yet he will be making gods by the dozen.
—*Michel de Montaigne*

Man, an ingenious assembly of portable plumbing.
—*Christopher Morley*

Man is the only animal that can remain on friendly terms with the victims he intends to eat until he eats them.
—*Samuel Butler*

The only time a woman really succeeds in changing a man is when he's a baby.
—*Natalie Wood*

MANAGEMENT
Lots of folks confuse bad management with destiny.
—*Frank McKinney Hubbard*

MANNERS
I don't recall your name, but your manners are familiar.
—*Oliver Herford*

The test of good manners is to be patient with bad ones.
—*Solomon Ibn Gabirol*

If a man has good manners and is not afraid of other people, he will get by even if he is stupid.
—*Sir David Eccles*

MARRIAGE

A good marriage would be between a blind wife and a deaf husband.
—*Michel de Montaigne*

Nowadays it's a happy marriage when the couple are as deeply in love as they are in debt.

We sleep in separate rooms; we have dinner apart; we take separate vacations. We're doing everything we can to keep our marriage together.
—*Rodney Dangerfield*

The most difficult years of marriage are those following the wedding.

Before marriage a man will lie awake all night thinking about something you said; after marriage he'll fall asleep before you finish saying it.
—*Helen Rowland*

A happy marriage is a long conversation that seems all too short.
—*André Maurois*

Marriage is an institution. Marriage is love. Love is blind. Therefore, marriage is an institution for the blind.

Marriage is a lottery, but you can't tear up your ticket if you lose.
—*F. M. Knowles*

Marriage is an institution where he rules the roost and she rules the rooster.

It resembles a pair of shears so joined that they cannot be separated, often moving in opposite directions, yet always punishing anyone who comes between them.
—*Sydney Smith*

The great secret of a successful marriage is to treat all disasters as incidents and none of the incidents as disasters.
—*Harold Nicholson*

My wife and I were happy for twenty years. Then we met.
—*Rodney Dangerfield*

The value of marriage is not that adults produce children but that children produce adults.
—*Peter De Vries*

If it weren't for marriage, men and women would have to fight with total strangers.

All marriages are happy. It's the living together afterward that causes all the trouble.

Before marriage a man declares he will be master in his own house or know the reason why; after marriage he knows the reason why.

MARRIAGE PROPOSALS

Hardly any woman reaches the age of thirty without having been asked to marry at least twice—once by her father, once by her mother.

MASS MEDIA

The mass media know their reports are worth nothing compared to the eye and voice of a serious writer. Like cowardly bulls, people in the mass media paw the ground when one comes near.
—*Norman Mailer*

MATHEMATICS

Mathematics—a wonderful science, but it hasn't yet come up with a way to divide one tricycle between three small boys.
—*Earl Wilson*

MEANNESS

Remember, the end never really justifies the meanness.

MEDITATION

My son has taken up meditation. At least it's better than sitting around doing nothing.

MEMORY

Memory is the diary we all carry about with us.
—*Oscar Wilde*

Memory is a marvelous thing—it enables you to
remember a mistake each time you repeat it.
—*Max Kauffmann*

When I was younger, I could remember anything,
whether it had happened or not.
—*Mark Twain*

"I did that," says my memory. "I could not have
done that," says my pride, and remains inexorable.
Eventually—the memory yields.
—*Friedrich Wilhelm*

I write down everything I want to remember. That
way, instead of spending a lot of time trying to
remember what it is I wrote down, I spend the
time looking for the paper I wrote it down on.
—*Beryl Pfizer*

Own only what you can always carry with you:
Know languages, know countries, know people.
Let your memory be your travel bag.
—*Aleksandr Solzhenitsyn*

MEN

Men are not against you; they are merely for themselves.
—*Gene Fowler*

Men are not flattered by being shown that there has been a difference of purpose between the Almighty and them.
—*Abraham Lincoln*

Men are nervous of remarkable women.
—*James M. Barrie*

MIDAS TOUCH

She had the Midas touch. Everything she touched turned into a muffler.
—*Lisa Smerling*

MIDDLE AGE

Middle age is when you've met so many people that every new person you meet reminds you of someone else.
—*Ogden Nash*

Middle age has arrived when a man's idea of get-up-and-go is going to bed.

Middle age is when a man figures he has enough financial security to wear the flashy sports coats he didn't have the courage to wear when he was young.
—*Bill Vaughan*

Middle age is when your age starts to show around your middle.
—*Bob Hope*

Middle age is when you burn the midnight oil around 9 P.M.

Middle age is the time of life when a man starts blaming the cleaners because his suits are shrinking.

Middle age is when you hope nobody will invite you out next Saturday night.

Middle age is the period when a woman's hair starts turning from gray to black.

Middle age is the time in life when you are determined to cut down on your calories—one of these days.

Don't worry about middle age; you'll outgrow it.

MIDDLE OF THE ROAD
We all know what happens to people who stay in the middle of the road. They get run over.

The middle of the road is where the yellow line is—and that's the worst place to drive.

MILK AND HONEY
The land of milk and honey has its drawbacks: You can get kicked by a cow and stung by a bee.

MILLIONAIRES
All a man has to do to become a millionaire in America is invent a low-calorie diet that tastes good.

MIMES

If you shoot a mime, should you use a silencer?

MIND

The mind is like a TV set: When it goes blank, it's a good idea to turn off the sound.

MINOR OPERATIONS

A minor operation is one that was performed on someone else.

MIRTH

Mirth is God's medicine.
—*Henry Ward Beecher*

MISERS

A miser is a guy who lives within his income. He's also called a magician.

MISSING LINK

The evolutionists seem to know everything about the missing link except the fact that it is missing.
—*G. K. Chesterton*

MISTAKES

The man who boasts he never made a mistake is often married to a woman who did.

When you make a mistake, admit it. If you don't, you only make matters worse.
—*Ward Cleaver*

Learn from the mistakes of others, because you can't live long enough to make them all by yourself.

Show me a man who makes no mistakes, and I will show you a man who doesn't do things.
—*Theodore Roosevelt*

In order to profit from your mistakes, you have to get out and make some.
—*Leroy B. Houghton*

The physician can bury his mistakes, but the architect can only advise his clients to plant vines.
—*Frank Lloyd Wright*

Wise men learn by other men's mistakes, fools by their own.

The man who makes no mistakes usually does not make anything,

MODESTY

Modesty is the only sure bait when you angle for praise.
—*Lord Chesterfield*

MONEY

I once had money and a friend;
My friend was short of cash.
I lent my money to my friend.
(Did I do something rash?)
I sought my money from my friend,
Which I had wanted long.
I lost my money and my friend.
(Did I do something wrong?)

When your outgo exceeds your income, your upkeep will be your downfall.

Not many Americans have been around the world, but their money sure has.
—*Walter Slezak*

If you would know the value of money, go and try to borrow some.
—*Benjamin Franklin*

No man's credit is as good as his money.
—*Henry Van Dyke*

Money may not buy friends, but it certainly gives you a better class of enemies.

Two can live as cheaply as one—and today they have to.

Two can live as cheaply as one—for half as long.

Today a dollar saved is a quarter earned.

Among the things that money can't buy is what it used to.
—*Max Kauffmann*

If you have money, you are wise and good-looking and can sing well, too.

Those who set out to serve both God and mammon soon discover that there is no God.
—*Logan Pearsall Smith*

Never ask of money spent
Where the spender thinks it went.
Nobody was ever meant
To remember or invent
What he did with every cent.
—*Robert Frost*

Money can't buy happiness, but it helps you to look for it in many more places.

Money may not buy happiness, but with it you can be unhappy in comfort.

Money talks, but most of us can't keep it long enough to hear what it says.

Money talks—it says good-bye.

Nobody works as hard for his money as the man who marries it.
—*Frank McKinney Hubbard*

A fool may make money, but it needs a wise man to spend it.
—*Charles Spurgeon*

Put your hand quickly to your hat and slowly to your purse.
—*Danish Proverb*

Men who are ashamed of the way their fathers made their money are never ashamed to spend it.

MONSTERS
Whoever fights monsters should see to it that in the process he does not become a monster. And when you look long into an abyss, the abyss also looks into you.
—*Friedrich Nietzsche*

MORNING
The horror of getting up is unparalleled, and I am filled with amazement every morning when I find that I have done it.
—*Lytton Strachey*

MOTHERS-IN-LAW
Have I got a mother-in-law. She's so neat she puts paper under the cuckoo clock.
—*Henny Youngman*

There are only three basic jokes, but since the mother-in-law joke is not a joke but a very serious question, there are only two.
—*George Ade*

Adam was the luckiest man: He had no mother-in-law.
—*Mark Twain*

MOTIVATION
The motivation that makes some women keep in shipshape is other women who are seeworthy.

Those who think they can't are generally right.

MOUNTAIN CLIMBERS
Mountain climbers always rope themselves together, probably to prevent the sensible ones from going home.

MOVIES
The movie was so bad that people were standing in line to get out.

MUD
He who slings mud generally loses ground.

MULES
You can't make a racehorse out of a mule.

MUSIC

Too many pieces of music finish too long after the end.
—*Igor Stravinsky*

The music at a wedding procession always reminds me of the music of soldiers going into battle.
—*Heinrich Heine*

MYSTERIES

One of life's greatest mysteries is how the boy who wasn't good enough to marry your daughter can be the father of the smartest grandchild in the world.

One of the mysteries of human conduct is why adult men and women are ready to sign documents they do not read, at the behest of salesmen they do not know, binding them to pay for articles they do not want, with money they do not have.
—*Gerald Hurst*

NAMES

I can't remember your name, but don't tell me.
—*Alexander Woolicott*

I can't remember your name, but your breath is familiar.

The sweetest sound to anyone's ear is the sound of his own name.
—*Dale Carnegie*

I think it is a terrible thing to go around dropping names, as the president remarked to me this last week.

NATIONAL BIRD

Our national bird is the eagle, with the stork a close second.

NECESSITY

Start doing what's necessary, then what's possible, and suddenly you are doing the impossible.
—*St. Francis of Assisi*

Necessity, my friend, is the mother of courage, as of invention.
—*Sir Walter Scott*

NECKTIES

Neckties strangle clear thinking.

NEIGHBORS

Don't talk about your neighbors; if your jaw needs exercise, chew gum.

NERVOUS BREAKDOWNS

Most of us are pretty good at postponing our nervous breakdowns until we can afford them.

NEUROTICS

A psychotic thinks that $2 + 2 = 5$. A neurotic knows that $2 + 2 = 4$. He just can't stand it.

Neurotic means he is not as sensible as I am, and psychotic means he's even worse than my brother-in-law.
—*Karl Menninger*

NEVER DIE

Old jokes never die; they just sound that way.

Old ladies never die; they just play bingo.

Old landlords sometimes die but are quickly replaced with real estate management companies.

Old mailmen never die; they just lose their zip.

Old physicians never die; they just lose their patients.

Old refrigerators never die; they just lose their cool.

Old rock hounds never die; they just petrify.

Old salesmen never die; they just go out of commission.

Old textbooks never die; they just get para-phrased.

NEWS
How can news be old?

NEWSPAPERS
Everything you read in the newspaper is absolutely true, except for that rare story of which you happen to have firsthand knowledge.
—*Erwin Knoll*

I read the newspaper avidly. It is my one form of continuous fiction.
—*Aneurin Bevan*

He had been kicked in the head by a mule when young and believed everything he read in the Sunday papers.
—*George Ade*

I do not take a single newspaper nor read one a month, and I feel myself infinitely the happier for it.
—*Thomas Jefferson*

The art of newspaper paragraphing is to stroke a platitude until it purrs like an epigram.
—*Don Marquis*

The man who never looks into a newspaper is better informed than he who reads them, inasmuch as he who knows nothing is nearer the truth than he whose mind is filled with falsehoods and errors.
—*Thomas Jefferson*

I keep reading between the lies.
—*Goodman Ace*

"The papers are not always reliable," Lincoln interjected. "That is to say, Mr. Welles, they lie and then they re-lie."
—*Carl Sandburg*

I became a newspaperman. I hated to do it, but I couldn't find honest employment.
—*Mark Twain*

NICENESS

It's amazing how nice people are to you when they know you're going away.
—*Michael Arlen*

NOAH

I was told by a person who said that he was studying for the ministry that even Noah got no salary for the first six months—partly on account of the weather and partly because he was learning navigation.
—*Mark Twain*

NOBODY

Who is wise? He that learns from everyone.
Who is powerful? He that governs his passions.
Who is rich? He that is content.
Who is that? Nobody.
—*Benjamin Franklin*

NOBODY CARES

If you think nobody cares if you're alive, try missing a couple of car payments.
—*Earl Wilson*

NOISE

Noise proves nothing. Often a hen who has merely laid an egg cackles as if she laid an asteroid.
—*Mark Twain*

NOSTALGIA

Nostalgia isn't what it used to be.

NOTHING

He who says nothing never lies.

I started out with nothing. I still have most of it.
—*Michael Davis*

When you have nothing to say, say nothing.
—*Charles Colton*

NOVELS

This is not a novel to be tossed aside lightly. It should be thrown with great force.

A good novel tells the truth about its hero; but a bad novel tells us the truth about its author.
—*G. K. Chesterton*

There are three rules for writing the novel. Unfortunately, no one knows what they are.
—*W. Somerset Maugham*

NUTS

The nut doesn't fall far from its tree.

OBITUARIES

Everybody is a potential murderer. I've never killed anyone, but I frequently get satisfaction reading the obituary notices.
—*Clarence Darrow*

OBNOXIOUSNESS

Arrogant, pompous, obnoxious, vain, cruel, persecuting, distasteful, verbose, a show-off. I have been called all of these. Of course I am.
—*Howard Cosell*

OBSCURITY

The distance from obscurity to fame is much longer than from fame to obscurity.

OCTOPUSES

What's worse than an octopus with tennis elbow? A centipede with athlete's foot.

OLD AGE

You'll know you're old when everything hurts and what doesn't hurt doesn't work.
—*George Burns*

My, my—sixty-five! I guess this marks the first day of the rest of our life savings.

He's so old his blood type was discontinued.

Anyone can get old. All you have to do is live long enough.
—*Groucho Marx*

You know you're getting older when the happy hour is a nap.

The greatest problem about old age is the fear that it may go on too long.

For the ignorant, old age is winter; for the learned, it is the harvest.

When I was younger, I could remember anything, whether it happened or not; but my faculties are decaying now, and soon I shall be so that I cannot remember anything but the things that never happened. It is sad to go to pieces like this, but we all have to do it.
—*Mark Twain*

OLDER GENERATION
The older generation thinks nothing of getting up at six in the morning—and the younger generation doesn't think much of it either.

OLD JOKES
If Adam were on earth again, the only thing he would recognize would be the old jokes and quotes.

OLD LETTERS

One of the pleasures of reading old letters is the knowledge that they need no answer.
—*Lord Byron*

ONCE UPON A TIME . . .

No more powerful, alluring words have ever been invented by the human race than these four: "Once upon a time. . . ."

ONE THING

The quickest way to do many things is to do only one thing at a time.

OPERA

People are wrong when they say that opera is not what it used to be. It is what it used to be. That is what is wrong with it.
—*Noel Coward*

Opera is when a guy gets stabbed in the back, and instead of bleeding, he sings.
—*Ed Gardner*

OPINIONS

Nobody agrees with the opinion of others; one merely agrees with one's own opinion expressed by others.

It is a difference of opinion that makes horse races.
—*Mark Twain*

OPPORTUNITIES

We are continually faced with a series of great opportunities brilliantly disguised as insoluble problems.
—*John W. Gardner*

Opportunities are usually disguised as hard work, so most people don't recognize them.

Keep yourself from opportunity, and God will keep you from sins.

When opportunity knocks, some people wait for it to break the door down and come in.

OPPOSITION

You can measure a man by the opposition it takes to discourage him.
—*Robert C. Savage*

OPTIMISTS

The optimist makes his own heaven and enjoys it as he goes through life. The pessimist makes his own hell and suffers as he goes through life.
—*William C. Hunter*

An optimist is a man who will wink at a pretty girl and think that his wife won't see him.

An optimist is a man who hurries because he thinks his date is waiting for him.

ORDEALS

Many a woman who marries her ideal soon discovers that he's her ordeal.

ORDERLINESS

Those proud of keeping an orderly desk never know the thrill of finding something they thought they had irretrievably lost.
—*Helen Exley*

An orderly desk is the sign of a sick mind.

ORIGINALITY

Your manuscript is both good and original; but the part that is good is not original, and the part that is original is not good.
—*Samuel Johnson*

Originality is the art of concealing your sources.

ORPHANS

At six I was left an orphan. What on earth is a six-year-old supposed to do with an orphan?

He reminds me of the man who murdered both of his parents, and then when sentence was about to be pronounced pleaded for mercy on the grounds that he was an orphan.
—*Abraham Lincoln*

OTHERS

At twenty we worry about what others think of us; at forty we don't care about what others think of us; at sixty we discover they haven't been thinking about us at all.

We would worry less about what others think of us if we realized how little they do.

If I am like others, who will be like me?

OUR TOWN

Here's to our town—a place where people spend money they haven't earned to buy things they don't need to impress people they don't like.
—*Lewis C. Henry*

OWLS

Owls are not really wise—they only look that way. The owl is a sort of college professor.
—*Elbert Hubbard*

PAIRS

We wear a pair of pants but never a pair of shirts.

PARADISE LOST

Paradise Lost is a book that, once put down, is very hard to pick up again.
—*Samuel Johnson*

PARANOIA

I told my psychiatrist that everyone hates me. He said I was being ridiculous—everyone hasn't met me yet.
—*Rodney Dangerfield*

PARKING

Don't complain about the traffic: If there were fewer cars on the road, it would be even harder to find a parking place.

He who does not remember the past forgets where he parked his car.

PATIENCE

Lack of pep is often mistaken for patience.
—*Frank McKinney Hubbard*

Beware the fury of a patient man.
—*John Dryden*

PAVLOV
Does the name Pavlov ring a bell?

PEACE AND QUIET
A phoneless cord—for people who like peace and quiet.

PEACE OF MIND
Peace of mind is better than giving them "a piece of your mind."
—*J. P. McEvoy*

PEDESTALS
The practice of putting women on pedestals began to die out when men discovered that women could give orders better from that position.

PEDESTRIANS
In some parts of the world, people still pray in the streets. In this country they're called pedestrians.
—*Gloria Pitzer*

PEDIGREE
Generally when a man brags about his pedigree, he has nothings else to brag about.

PEOPLE

It is absurd to divide people into good and bad.
People are either charming or tedious.
—*Oscar Wilde*

People are like plants: Some go to seed with age,
and others to pot.

PERHAPS

A pinch of probably is worth a pound of perhaps.
—*James Thurber*

PERMISSIVENESS

Permissiveness is the principle of treating children
as if they were adults and the tactic of making sure
they never reach that stage.
—*Thomas Szasz*

PESSIMISTS

A lot of people become pessimists from financing
optimists.
—*C. T. Jones*

PHD'S

The average PhD thesis is nothing but the trans-
ference of bones from one graveyard to another.
—*J. Frank Dobie*

PHILOSOPHERS

There is no opinion so absurd that some philosopher will not express it.

I have tried in my time to be a philosopher; but I don't know how, cheerfulness was always breaking in.
—*Oliver Edwards*

There is no record in human history of a happy philosopher.

PHONE CALLS

For three days after death, hair and fingernails continue to grow, but phone calls taper off.
—*Johnny Carson*

PHYSICAL FITNESS

As a nation we are dedicated to keeping physically fit—and parking as close to the stadium as possible.
—*Bill Vaughan*

PHYSICIANS

We may lay it down as a maxim that when a nation abounds in physicians it grows thin of people.
—*Joseph Addison*

The blunders of physicians are covered by the earth.

I die by the help of too many physicians.
—*Alexander the Great*

Physicians think they do a lot for a patient when they give his disease a name.
—*Immanuel Kant*

PICKING UP THE TAB
It may be expensive to reach for the check, but it gets you home earlier.

PITY
Better to be envied than pitied.
—*Herodotus*

PLAGIARISM
If you steal from one author, it's plagiarism; if you steal from many, it's research.
—*Wilson Mizner*

PLAYS
I didn't like the play, but then I saw it under adverse conditions: The curtain was up.
—*Groucho Marx*

It was the sort of play that gives failures a bad name.
—*Walter Kerr*

It was one of those plays in which the actors, unfortunately, enunciated very clearly.
—*Robert Benchley*

PLEASURE

The great pleasure in life is doing what people say you cannot do.
—*Walter Bagehot*

Follow pleasure, and then will pleasure flee,
Flee pleasure, and pleasure will follow thee.
—*John Heywood*

PLEDGES

To make a pledge of any kind is to declare war against nature; for a pledge is a chain that is always clanking and reminding the wearer of it that he is not a free man.
—*Mark Twain*

POEMS

My favorite poem is the one that starts "Thirty days hath September" because it actually tells you something.
—*Groucho Marx*

Robert Creeley's poems have two main characteristics: (1) They are short; (2) they are not short enough.
—*John Simon*

Publishing a volume of verse is like dropping a rose petal down the Grand Canyon and waiting for the echo.
—*Don Marquis*

Then he asked the question that you are all itching to ask me: "How can you tell good poetry from bad?" I answered: "How does one tell good fish from bad? Surely by the smell. Use your nose."
—*Robert Graves*

POETS

Poets all have imagination because they imagine people are going to read their poems.

POLITENESS

Politeness: the most acceptable hypocrisy.
—*Ambrose Bierce*

POLITICIANS

I know a politician who believes that there are two sides to every question—and takes them both.
—*Ken Murray*

Figures don't lie, except political figures.

An honest politician is one who when he is bought will stay bought.
—*Simon Cameron*

Since a politician never believes what he says, he is surprised when others believe him.
—*Charles de Gaulle*

Instead of giving a politician the keys to the city, it might be better to change the locks.
—*Doug Larson*

A politician is a man who approaches every question with an open mouth.
—*Adlai Stevenson*

When a politician is on the fence, the fence is really a hedge.

I find honorary degrees always tempting, and often bad for me: tempting because we all—even ex-politicians—hope to be mistaken for scholars, and bad because if you then make a speech, the mistake is quickly exposed.
—*Adlai Stevenson*

Ninety percent of the politicians give the other 10 percent a bad reputation.
—*Henry Kissinger*

POLITICS

Politics is perhaps the only profession for which no preparation is thought necessary.
—*Robert Louis Stevenson*

I looked up the word politics in the dictionary, and it's actually a combination of two words: poli, which means "many" and tics, which means "bloodsuckers."
—*Jay Leno*

POSITIVE

Positive: being mistaken at the top of one's voice.
—*Ambrose Bierce*

POSTAGE STAMPS

We cannot put the face of a person on a stamp unless said person is deceased. My suggestion, therefore, is that you drop dead.
—*James Edward Day*

POVERTY

One thing you can say for poverty—it's inexpensive.

I used to think I was poor. Then they told me I wasn't poor, I was needy. Then they told me it was self-defeating to think of myself as needy, I was deprived. Then they told me that underprivileged was overused. I was disadvantaged. I still don't have a dime. But I have a great vocabulary.
—*Jules Feiffer*

The rich get richer, and the poor get children.

The advantage of being poor is that a doctor will cure you faster.

POWER

Nearly all men can stand adversity, but if you want to test a man's character, give him power.
—Abraham Lincoln

I am more and more convinced that man is a dangerous creature and that power, whether vested in many or a few, is ever grasping and like the grace, cries, "Give, give."
—Abigail Adams

Power intoxicates men. When a man is intoxicated by alcohol, he can recover, but when he is intoxicated by power, he seldom recovers.
—James F. Byrnes

PRACTICE

If you think practice makes perfect, you don't have a child taking piano lessons.

PRAISE

The advantage of doing one's praising for oneself is that one can lay it on so thick and exactly in the right places.
—Samuel Butler

We run ourselves down so as to be praised by others.
—*François La Rochefoucauld*

Try praising your wife even if it does frighten her
at first.
—*Billy Sunday*

PRAYER

There are only two occasions when Americans
respect privacy, especially in presidents. Those
are prayer and fishing. So that some have taken to
fishing.
—*Herbert Hoover*

Some people will say anything except their
prayers.

PREACHERS

When I hear a man preach, I like to see him act as
if he were fighting bees.
—*Abraham Lincoln*

He charged nothing for his preaching, and it was
worth it, too.
—*Mark Twain*

PREJUDICE

Prejudice is never easy unless it can pass itself off
for reason.
—*William Hazlitt*

One may no more live in the world without picking up the moral prejudices of the world than one will be able to go to hell without perspiring.
—*H. L. Mencken*

A prejudiced person is one who doesn't believe in the same things we do.
—*Art Linkletter*

PRESERVATIVES
Old people shouldn't eat health foods. They need all the preservatives they can get.
—*Robert Orben*

PRIDE
There is a paradox in pride: It makes some men ridiculous but prevents others from becoming so.
—*C. C. Colton*

Pride is at the bottom of all great mistakes.
—*John Ruskin*

When a man is wrapped up in himself, he makes a pretty small package.
—*John Ruskin*

PRINCIPLES
It is easier to fight for one's principles than to live up to them.
—*Alfred Adler*

PRIVILEGE

It is the privilege of adults to give advice. It is the privilege of youth not to listen. Both avail themselves of their privileges, and the world rocks along.
—*D. Sutten*

PROBLEMS

It is easy to bear another person's problems.

I have problems flown in fresh daily wherever I am.
—*Richard Lewis*

The significant problems we face cannot be solved at the same level of thinking we were at when we created them.
—*Albert Einstein*

PROFESSIONALISM

A professional is a man who can do his job when he doesn't feel like it. An amateur is a man who can't do his job when he does feel like it.
—*James Agate*

PROJECTS

Don't undertake a project unless it is manifestly important and nearly impossible.
—*Edwin H. Land*

PROMISES

A man apt to promise is apt to forget.
—*Thomas Fuller*

Promise little and do much.

Promises may make friends, but 'tis performances that keep them.

Some men divide their time equally: one half making promises, one half making excuses. If you make no promises, you'll need no excuses and can then devote all your time to getting business.
—*William C. Hunter*

PSYCHIATRISTS

If you are suffering from paranoia, everyone will tell you about it.

You go to a psychiatrist when you're slightly cracked and keep going until you're completely broke.

A neurotic is a man who builds a castle in the air.
A psychotic is the man who lives in it.
A psychiatrist is the man who collects the rent.

I do not have a psychiatrist, and I do not want one for the simple reason that if he listened to me long enough, he might become disturbed.
—*James Thurber*

Mad money is the fee charged by psychiatrists.

A psychiatrist is a fellow who asks you a lot of expensive questions your wife asks for nothing.

Anybody who goes to see a psychiatrist ought to have his head examined.
—*Samuel Goldwyn*

A psychiatrist is the next man you start talking to after you start talking to yourself.
—*Fred Allen*

Advice to psychiatrists: In treating cases of amnesia, collect the fee in advance.

Psychiatry enables us to correct our faults by confessing our parents' shortcomings.
—*Laurence Peter*

I gave up visiting my psychoanalyst because he was meddling too much in my private life.
—*Tennessee Williams*

PSYCHOLOGY
He knew the precise psychological moment when to say nothing.
—*Oscar Wilde*

PUNCTUALITY
Punctuality is the virtue of the bored.
—*Evelyn Waugh*

Punctuality: the art of guessing correctly how late the other party is going to be.

PUNS

A pun is the lowest form of humor—when you don't think of it first.
—*Oscar Levant*

I never knew an enemy to puns who was not an ill-natured man.
—*Charles Lamb*

Of puns it has been said that they who most dislike them are least able to utter them.
—*Edgar Allan Poe*

The inveterate punster follows a conversation as a shark follows a ship.
—*Stephen Leacock*

PUPPIES

The best way to get a puppy is to beg for a baby brother—they'll settle for a puppy every time.
—*Winston Pendelton*

QUARRELS

The only people who listen to both sides of a family quarrel are the next-door neighbors.

Quarreling is like cutting water with a sword.

QUESTIONS

To a quick question, give a slow answer.

There are two sides to every question that we are not interested in.

There are two sides to every question, otherwise it would not be a question.

Avoid a questioner, for such a man is also a tattler.
—*Horace*

RACEHORSES

A racehorse is the only creature that can take thousands of people for a ride at the same time.

If fifty thousand people ran daily at a race track, not one horse would attend.

RADICALS

A radical is a man with both feet firmly planted in the air.

—*Franklin Delano Roosevelt*

RAGE

Don't fly into a rage unless you are prepared for a rough landing.

RAINBOWS

When I was a kid, I was so poor that in my neighborhood the rainbow was black and white.

—*Rodney Dangerfield*

The way I see it, if you want the rainbow, you gotta put up with the rain.

—*Dolly Parton*

RATS

He bears an unmistakable resemblance to a cornered rat.

—*Norman Mailer*

The trouble with the rat race is that even if you win, you're still a rat.
—*Lily Tomlin*

READING

Read the best books first, or you may not have a chance to read them at all.
—*Henry David Thoreau*

There is a great deal of difference between the eager man who wants to read a book and the tired man who wants a book to read.
—*G. K. Chesterton*

He has left off reading altogether, to the great improvement of his originality.
—*Charles Lamb*

REALISTS

You may be sure that when a man begins to call himself a realist, he is preparing to do something that he is secretly ashamed of doing.
—*Sydney J. Harris*

REASON

The best way to get someone to listen to reason is to mix some flattery with it.

REASONS

There's always a good reason, and then there's the real reason.

A man's acts are usually right, but his reasons seldom are.

Give your decisions, never your reasons; your decisions may be right, but your reasons are sure to be wrong.
—*William Murray*

REBELS

There comes a time when rebellious young people should take their turn as adults against whom the next wave of youngsters can rebel.
—*D. Sutten*

RECESSIONS

A recession is a period during which you discover how much money you were wasting on nonessentials.

REFRIGERATORS

A refrigerator is a place where you store leftovers until they are ready to be thrown out.

RELATIVES

God sends our relatives, but we can choose our friends.

RELATIVITY

When a man sits with a pretty girl for an hour, it seems like a minute. But let him sit on a hot stove for a minute—and it's longer than any hour. That's relativity.
—*Albert Einstein*

Everything is relative: You're expendable when you ask for a raise but indispensable when you ask for a day off.

RELIGION

Men will wrangle for religion, write for it, fight for it, die for it—anything but live for it.
—*C. C. Colton*

If men are so wicked with religion, what would they be without it?
—*Benjamin Franklin*

REMEDIES

For every evil under the sun,
There is a remedy or there is none.
If there is one, try and find it,
If there be none, never mind it.

REPARTEE

Repartee is a duel fought with the points of jokes.
—*Max Eastman*

Repartee is what you think of on the way home.

REPENTANCE
We withdraw our wrath from the man who admits that he is justly punished.
—*Aristotle*

Too late repents the rat when caught by the cat.
—*John Florio*

REPUTATION
Character is made by what you stand for; reputation, by what you fall for.
—*Robert Quillen*

The reputation of a thousand years may be determined by the conduct of one hour.

RESPECT
I was always taught to respect my elders, and I've reached the age when I don't have anybody to respect.
—*George Burns*

RESPONSIBILITY
Soon after I received my Acme pencil, it rolled off the desk and onto the floor. I bent over to pick it up and strained my back. On the way up I hit my head on the desk. Can I sue and hold Acme responsible?

REST

A day away from some people is like a month in
the country.
—*Howard Dietz*

RESTAURANT SERVICE

I'd complain about the service if I could find a
waiter to complain to.
—*Mel Calman*

RETIREMENT

Retirement means twice as much husband on half
as much money.

REVENGE

Forgetting of a wrong is mild revenge.
—*Thomas Fuller*

Revenge is often like biting a dog because the dog
bit you.
—*Austin O'Malley*

RICH

Don't knock the rich—when did a poor person
ever give you a job?

RICHES

The greatest luxury of riches is that they enable
you to escape so much good advice.
—*Sir Arthur Helps*

RIDICULE

There is no character, howsoever good and fine, but it can be destroyed by ridicule, howsoever poor and witless. Observe the mule, for instance: His character is about perfect, he is the choicest spirit among all the humbler animals, yet see what ridicule has done to him.

Ridicule is the deadliest of weapons against a lofty cause.
—*Samuel Hopkins Adams*

RIGHT

Lord, when we are wrong, make us willing to change. And when we are right, make us easy to live with.
—*Peter Marshall*

Always do right. This will gratify some people and astonish the rest.
—*Mark Twain*

RISK TAKING

Yes, risk taking is inherently failure-prone. Otherwise, it would be called sure-thing-taking.
—*Tim McMahon*

ROADS

It's a short road that somebody hasn't written a song about.

The road to hell is always in good repair because its users pay so dearly for its upkeep.

ROCK JOURNALISM

Most rock journalism is people who cannot write interviewing people who cannot talk for people who cannot read.
—*Frank Zappa*

ROCK 'N' ROLL

The greatest line in rock 'n' roll is, "Awopbo-paloobop Alopbamboom." Top that if you can!
—*Wilko Johnson*

ROOSTERS

A good rooster crows in any henhouse.
—*Frank C. Brown*

ROSES

Why is it no one ever sent me yet
One perfect limousine, do you suppose?
Ah, no, it's always just my luck to get
One perfect rose.
—*Dorothy Parker*

ROWE'S RULE

Rowe's rule: The odds are 5 to 6 that the light at the end of the tunnel is the headlight of an oncoming train.
—*Paul Dickson*

RUTS

The only difference between a rut and a grave is their dimensions.
—*Ellen Glasgow*

SACRIFICE

Virtue does not always demand heavy sacrifice—
only the willingness to make it when necessary.

SADNESS

No one is more profoundly sad than he who
laughs too much.

For of all sad words of tongue or pen,
The saddest are these: "It might have been."
—*John Greenleaf Whittier*

SAINTS

A bad man is worse when he pretends to be a
saint.
—*Francis Bacon*

SALES

The clergy can do nothing about rainy Sundays;
they are in sales, not in management.

SANITY

I suppose it is much more comfortable to be mad
and not know it than to be sane and have one's
doubts.
—*G. B. Burgin*

SANTA CLAUS

I stopped believing in Santa Claus when my mother took me to see him in a department store and he asked for my autograph.
—*Shirley Temple*

Santa Claus has the right idea: Visit people once a year.
—*Victor Borge*

SATISFACTION

There is no satisfaction in hanging a man who does not object to it.
—*George Bernard Shaw*

SAVE

Whenever you hear the word save, it is usually the beginning of an advertisement designed to make you spend money.

SAVED

Few sinners are saved after the first twenty minutes of a sermon.
—*Mark Twain*

SAVING

Saving is a very fine thing, especially when your parents have done it for you.
—*Winston Churchill*

SAVING FACE

If you want to save face, keep the lower half shut.

SCALPERS

A ticket scalper is a man who enables you to see one football game for the price of five.

SCARE

A good scare is worth more to a man than good advice.
—*E. W. Howe*

SCHOOL BUS DRIVERS

Everyone is in awe of the lion tamer in a cage with a half-dozen lions—everyone but a school bus driver.

SCIENCE

When science finishes getting man up to the moon, maybe it can have another try at getting pigeons down from public buildings.

SCREENS

Screens: the wire mesh that keeps flies from getting out of the house.
—*Abe Martin*

SCRIPTURE

Most people are bothered by those passages of Scripture they do not understand. . . . The passages that bother me are those I do understand.
—*Mark Twain*

SCULPTORS

You show me a sculptor who works in the basement, and I'll show you a low-down chiseler.

SEAFOOD DIET

I'm on a seafood diet. I see food, and I eat it.

SEASICK

We all like to see people seasick when we are not ourselves.
—*Mark Twain*

SECRETS

Whoever wishes to keep a secret must hide the fact that he possesses one.
—*Johann von Goethe*

Two can keep a secret if one of them is dead. Three may keep a secret if two of them are dead.

The only way to keep a secret is to forget it.

If you wish to preserve your secret, wrap it up in frankness.
—*Alexander Smith*

A woman can keep one secret—the secret of her age.
—*Voltaire*

The proof that women can keep secrets better than men is that they can be engaged for months before telling their fiancés all about it.

SEEKING
Seek and ye shall find that a lot of other people are looking for the same thing.

SELF-DECEPTION
Self-deception is the first law of human nature.

SELF-INTEREST
Poke any saint deeply enough, and you touch self-interest.
—*Irving Wallace*

SELF-MADE MEN
He is a self-made man and worships his creator.
—*John Bright*

He is a self-made man, which shows what happens when you don't follow the directions.

SERENITY

God, give us the grace to accept with serenity the things that cannot be changed, courage to change the things which should be changed, and the wisdom to distinguish the one from the other.
—*Reinhold Niebuhr*

SETTLEMENT

Any time a man can't come and settle with you without bringing his lawyer—look out for him.
—*Will Rogers*

SEWAGE

She poured a little social sewage into his ears.
—*George Meredith*

SHAMEFUL

Harmless is the opposite of harmful, but shame-less and shameful are the same.

SHEEP

Make yourself into a sheep, and you'll meet a wolf nearby.

He is a sheep in sheep's clothing.
—*Sir Winston Churchill*

SHINS

A shin is a device for finding furniture in the dark.

SHOPPING

When the going gets tough, the tough go shopping.

I feel like such a failure. I've been shopping for over twenty years, and I still have nothing to wear.

SHORT MEN

It's better to have loved a short man than never to have loved a tall.

SIGNS

Question on church sign board: This Is a Ch——ch. What Is Missing? U-R.

Sign on sanitarium: Nobody Leaves Here Mad.

Sign in church vestibule: "If you were on trial for being a Christian, would there be enough evidence to convict you?"

SILENCE

Silence isn't always golden; sometimes it's just plain yellow.

The fact that silence is golden may explain why there is so little of it.

Silence: the unbearable repartee.
—*G. K. Chesterton*

Silence is one of the hardest arguments to refute.
—*Josh Billings*

Silence is not always tact, and it is tact that is golden, not silence.
—*Samuel Butler*

There is no point in speaking unless you can improve on silence.

Saying nothing indicates a fine command of the English language.

Silence can't be misquoted.

Sometimes you have to be silent to be heard.

SIMPLE THINGS
Most girls are attracted to the simple things in life, like men.

SIN
The wages of sin is an income for life.

Every sin is the result of a collaboration.
—*Stephen Crane*

There is no sin without previous preparation.

Sin has always been an ugly word, but it has been made so in a new sense over the last half century. It has been made not only ugly but passé. People are no longer sinful. They are only immature or underprivileged or frightened or, more particularly, sick.
—*Phyllis McGinley*

SINCERITY
He has the ability to be sincere without being honest.
—*Clemet Greenberg*

SINGING
I can't sing. As a singist I am not a success. I am saddest when I sing. So are those who hear me. They are sadder even than I am.
—*Charles Farrar Browne*

SITTING
Sometimes I sits and thinks, and sometimes I just sits.

I do most of my work sitting down; that's where I shine.
—*Robert Benchley*

SKUNKS

It doesn't pay to fight with a skunk because if you
win, you lose.

It doesn't pay to fight with a skunk, you may win
but you will come out smelling something awful.
—*Abraham Lincoln*

SLEEP

Most people spend their lives going to bed when
they're not sleepy and getting up when they are!
—*Cindy Adams*

SMALL TOWNS

It was such a small town that we didn't even have
a village idiot. We had to take turns.

The town was so small it had only one yellow page.

SMILES

Don't open a shop unless you like to smile.
—*Chinese Proverb*

SMOKING

As ye smoke, so shall ye reek.

To cease smoking is the easiest thing I ever did;
I ought to know because I've done it a thousand
times.
—*Mark Twain*

I will grant, here, that I have stopped smoking now and then for a few months at a time, but it was not on principle—it was only to show off; it was to pulverize those critics who said I was a slave to my habits and couldn't break my bonds.
—*Mark Twain*

Smoking is one of the leading causes of statistics.

Smoking won't send you to hell; it only makes it smell like you've been there.

SNOBS
Snobs talk as if they had begotten their ancestors.
—*Herbert Agar*

SNORING
Laugh, and the world laughs with you; snore, and you sleep alone.

SOCIOLOGISTS
The parable of the Good Samaritan for sociologists: A man was attacked and left bleeding in a ditch. Two sociologists passed by, and one said to the other, "We must find the man who did this—he needs help."

SOFTNESS OF HEAD

I think there is only one quality worse than hardness of heart, and that is softness of head.
—*Theodore Roosevelt*

SOLITUDE

Solitude is a good place to visit but a poor place to stay.
—*Josh Billings*

SOLUTIONS

I don't have any solution, but I certainly admire the problem.

SONS

At five years of age, your son is your master, at ten your slave, at fifteen your double, and after that your friend or foe.

SORROW

Sorrow is like a precious treasure, shown only to friends.

It's a short way from happiness to sorrow but a long way from sorrow to happiness.

SPEAKERS

Some speakers electrify their listeners; others only gas them.
—*Sidney Smith*

Fill your mouth with marbles, and make a speech. Every day reduce the number of marbles in your mouth, and make a speech. You will soon become an accredited public speaker—as soon as you have lost all your marbles.
—*Brooks Hays*

SPEAKING

The ability to speak several languages is an asset, but the ability to keep your mouth shut in one language is priceless.

Think twice before you speak and then talk to yourself.

Never speak ill of yourself; your friends will always say enough on that subject.
—*Charles Talleyrand*

SPECULATION

There are two times in a man's life when he should not speculate: when he can't afford it, and when he can.
—*Mark Twain*

SPEECHES

Three things matter in a speech—who says it, how he says it, and what he says—and of the three, the last matters the least.
—*John Morley*

The most popular after-dinner speech that any man can make is, "I'll wash the dishes."

If you don't say anything, you won't be called on to repeat it.
—*Calvin Coolidge*

If a thing goes without saying, let it.
—*Jacob M. Braude*

Speeches are like babies—easy to conceive but hard to deliver.
—*Pat O'Malley*

SPENDING

Don't think you can spend yourself rich.
—*George Humphrey*

SPITTING

He who spits against the wind spits in his own face.

I don't get angry, but where I spit the grass dies.

SPORTSWRITERS

If I ever needed a brain transplant, I'd choose
a sportswriter because I'd want a brain that had
never been used.
—*Norm Van Brocklin*

STATESMEN

The first requirement of a statesman is that he be
dull. This is not always easy to achieve.
—*Dean Acheson*

STATING THE OBVIOUS

I like the way you always manage to state the
obvious with a sense of real discovery.
—*Gore Vidal*

STATISTICS

He used statistics the way a drunkard uses lamp-
posts—for support, not illumination.
—*Andrew Lang*

In ancient times they had no statistics, so they had
to fall back on lies.
—*Stephen Leacock*

Statistics show what really happens if you exercise
daily—you die healthier.

STEALING

A man who has never gone to school may steal from a freight car; but if he has a university education, he may steal the whole railroad.
—*Theodore Roosevelt*

STEPPING ON TOES

The best way to keep from stepping on the other fellow's toes is to put yourself in his shoes.

STEPPING-STONES

The difference between stumbling blocks and stepping-stones is the way you use them.

STITCH IN TIME

A stitch in time saves embarrassment.

STOCK MARKET

If ignorance paid dividends, everyone would make a fortune in the stock market.

STORAGE

If you keep anything long enough, you can throw it away. If you throw it away, you will need it the next day.

STORYTELLING

The trouble with telling a good story is that it invariably reminds the other fellow of a bad one.

A good storyteller is a person who has a good memory and hopes other people haven't.

STRANGERS

I do desire we may be better strangers.
—*William Shakespeare*

STUPIDITY

The difference between genius and stupidity is that genius has its limits.

He was good-natured, obliging, and immensely ignorant and endowed with a stupidity which by the least little stretch would go around the globe four times and tie.
—*Mark Twain*

SUBURBIA

Suburbia is where the developer bulldozes out the trees, then names streets after them.
—*Bill Vaughn*

SUCCESS

If at first you do succeed, it's probably your father's business.

The worst part of having success is trying to find someone who is happy for you.

Behind every successful man there stands an amazed woman.

There's no secret about success. Did you ever know a successful man that didn't tell you all about it?
—*Frank McKinney Hubbard*

Success: the one unpardonable sin against one's fellows.
—*Ambrose Bierce*

All men want to succeed; some want to succeed so badly they're even willing to work for it.

Success is just a matter of luck. Ask any failure.
—*Earl Wilson*

The reason many people don't climb the ladder of success is that they're waiting for the elevator.

Anyone can sympathize with the sufferings of a friend, but it requires a very fine nature to sympathize with a friend's success.
—*Oscar Wilde*

Three things are needed for success: a backbone, a wishbone, and a funny bone.

Success has made failures of many men.

You don't have to lie awake nights to succeed—
just stay awake days.

SUFFERING
If you suffer, thank God! It is a sure sign that you
are alive.
—*Elbert Hubbard*

Although the world is full of suffering, it is full
also of the overcoming of it.
—*Helen Keller*

SUITS
The reason men's suits look the same year after
year is that most men are wearing the same ones.

SUNBURN
I never expected to see the day when girls would
get sunburned in the places they do now.
—*Will Rogers*

SUPERHIGHWAYS
Superhighway: a prison in motion.

SUSPENSE
Even cowards can endure hardship; only the brave
can endure suspense.
—*Mignon McLaughlin*

SUSPICION

If you would avoid suspicion, don't lace your shoes in a melon field.

SWEEPING

If everyone sweeps in front of his door, the whole city will be clean.

TACKS
It's a sure sign somebody has been thinking about you when you find a tack in your chair.

TAKE-HOME PAY
The trouble with take-home pay today is that it turns out to be just about enough to get you there.

TALENT
Another difference between talent and genius is that talent gets paid.

It is in the ability to deceive oneself that one shows the greatest talent.
—*Anatole France*

TALK
A child learns to talk in about two years, but it takes about sixty years for him to learn to keep his mouth shut.

Women eat while they are talking; men talk while they are eating.

A gossip is one who talks to you about others; a bore is one who talks to you about himself; and a brilliant conversationalist is one who talks to you about yourself.
—*Lisa Kirk*

Don't talk about yourself; it will be done when you leave.
—*Addison Mizner*

You may talk too much on the best of subjects.
—*Benjamin Franklin*

There is so much good in the worst of us,
And so much bad in the best of us,
That it hardly behooves any of us
To talk about the rest of us.

Two great talkers will not travel far together.
—*George Borrow*

Look out fer th' feller who lets you do all th' talkin'.
—*Frank McKinney Hubbard*

The opposite of talking isn't listening. The opposite of talking is waiting.

TAXES

I believe we should all pay our tax bill with a smile. I tried—but they wanted cash.

We have taxed our economy the way old-time doctors bled their patients, and with similar results.

If Patrick Henry thought that taxation without representation was bad, he should see how bad it is *with* representation.

There will always be two classes of people who don't like to pay income taxes: men and women.

With the state the world is in, any government could raise unlimited revenue simply by taxing sins.

The taxpayer—that's someone who works for the federal government but doesn't have to take a civil service examination.
—*Ronald Reagan*

Don't get excited about a tax cut. It's like a mugger giving you back fare for a taxi.
—*Arnold Glasow*

TEARS

The most effective water power in the world—women's tears.
—*Wilson Mizner*

TEENAGERS

Remember that as a teenager you are at the last stage in your life when you will be happy to hear that the phone is for you.
—*Fran Lebowitz*

When a teenager is watching television, listening to her CD player, and talking on the phone, she is probably doing her homework.

Don't tell a teenager that her hair looks like a mop; she probably doesn't know what a mop is.

There's nothing wrong with teenagers that reasoning with them won't aggravate.

TELEPHONES

What happens when the human body is completely submerged in water? The telephone rings.

TELEVISION

When you watch television, you never see people watching television. We love television because it brings us a world in which television does not exist.
—*Barbara Ehrenreich*

Television has done much for psychiatry by spreading information about it as well as contributing to the need for it.
—*Alfred Hitchcock*

Television is an invention that permits you to be entertained in your living room by people you wouldn't have in your home.
—*David Frost*

I wish there were a knob on the television so you could turn up the intelligence. They have one marked "brightness," but it doesn't work very well.

In general, my children refused to eat anything that hadn't danced on television.
—*Erma Bombeck*

Television—a medium. So called because it is neither rare nor well done.
—*Ernie Kovacs*

Nowadays early to bed and early to rise probably means the television set isn't working.

Television brings the family into the same room so that they can ignore each other close together.

TELL IT LIKE IT IS
We have enough people who tell it like it is—now we could use a few who tell it like it can be.
—*Robert Orben*

TEMPER
When you are right, you can afford to keep your temper, and when your are in the wrong, you cannot afford to lose it.

TEMPTATION
The biggest human temptation is . . . to settle for too little.
—*Thomas Merton*

Don't worry about avoiding temptation—as you grow older, it starts avoiding you.

Opportunity knocks but once, but temptation leans on the doorbell.

When you run from temptation, don't leave a forwarding address.

There are several good protections against temptation, but the surest is cowardice.
—*Mark Twain*

TEN COMMANDMENTS
Someone has tabulated that we have 35 million laws on the books to enforce the Ten Commandments.
—*Bert Masterson*

THANKFULNESS
If you can't be thankful for what you have, be thankful for what you have escaped.

THINKING
If you make people think they're thinking, they'll love you; but if you really make them think, they'll hate you.
—*Don Marquis*

Why can't somebody give us a list of things everybody thinks and nobody says and another list of things that everybody says and nobody thinks?
—*Oliver Wendell Holmes*

The man who says what he thinks is finished, and the man who thinks what he says is an idiot.
—*Rolf Hochhuth*

A great many people think they are thinking when they are merely rearranging their prejudices.
—*William James*

The only reason some people get lost in thought is because it's unfamiliar territory.

THINKING IT OVER
When a person tells you, "I'll think it over and let you know"—you know.
—*Olin Miller*

THREATS
Do not threaten a child; either punish or forgive him.

TIME
Killing time can be suicide.

I've been on a calendar but never on time.
—*Marilyn Monroe*

Who kills time murders opportunity.
—*Frederick H. Seymour*

If you've got time to kill, work it to death.

TIMES CHANGE

Times change: In the old days no one asked how many miles a horse did on a bundle of hay.

TIME WASTERS

The worst thing about time wasters is that so much of the time they waste what doesn't belong to them.

TOLERANCE

Tolerance is the ability to listen to a person describe the same ailment you have.

TOMBSTONES

Many a tombstone inscription is a grave error.

TONGUE

The tongue: We spend three years learning how to use it and the rest of our lives learning how to control it.

TOO BIG FOR HIS BRITCHES

He who gets too big for his britches gets exposed in the end.

TOURISTS

Tourists are alike: They all want to go places where there are not tourists.

TRAVEL

In America there are two classes of travel: first class and with children.
—*Robert Benchley*

If God meant for us to travel tourist class, he would have made us narrower.
—*Martha Zimmerman*

TROUBLE

If you're going looking for trouble, you don't need to get ready for a long trip.

Most of the trouble in the world is caused by people wanting to be important.
—*T. S. Eliot*

The capacity for getting into trouble and the ability for getting out of it are seldom combined in the same person.

Never trouble trouble till trouble troubles you.

Every horse thinks his own pack the heaviest.

Never go out to meet trouble. If you will just sit still, nine cases out of ten someone will intercept it before it reaches you.
—*Calvin Coolidge*

The wind in a man's face makes him wise.
—*John Ray*

The things that are hardest to bear are sweetest to remember.
—*Seneca*

Of all our troubles great and small,
The greatest are those that don't happen at all.

If winter comes, can spring be far behind?
—*Percy Bysshe Shelley*

Your neighbors' troubles are not as bad as yours, but their children are worse.

I have had troubles in my life, but the worst of them never came.
—*James A. Garfield*

TRUTH

If you tell the truth, you don't have to remember anything.
—*Mark Twain*

The absolute truth is the thing that makes people laugh.
—*Carl Reiner*

Telling the truth is a business in which there is very little competition.

Men occasionally stumble over the truth, but most of them pick themselves up and hurry off as if nothing had happened.
—*Winston Churchill*

A remark generally hurts in proportion to its truth.
—*Will Rogers*

Nowadays, truth is not only stranger than fiction, it's a lot cleaner.

Half the truth is often a great lie.

He who speaks the truth should have one foot in the stirrup.

A man that should call everything by its right name would hardly pass the streets without being knocked down as a common enemy.
—*Lord Halifax*

A man would rather have a hundred lies told of him than one truth which he does not wish should be told.
—*Samuel Johnson*

Truth always lags behind, limping along on the arm of time.
—*Baltasar Gracian*

The truth doesn't hurt unless it ought to.
—*B. C. Forbes*

Truth never dies but leads a tortured life.

UGLY
How can ugly be pretty?

UNCLE SAM
I figured out why Uncle Sam wears such a tall hat.
It comes in handy when he passes it around in
April.

UNDECIDED
Decided only to be undecided, resolved to be
irresolute, adamant for drift, solid for fluidity,
all-powerful to be impotent.
—*Winston Churchill*

Some problems are so complex that you have to
be highly intelligent and well informed just to be
undecided about them.
—*Laurence J. Peter*

UNDERSTANDING
If men talked about only what they understood,
the silence would become unbearable.
—*Max Lerner*

UNEMPLOYMENT
The trouble with unemployment is that the minute you wake up in the morning you're on the job.

UNEXPECTED

After the unexpected has happened, there is always someone who knew it would.

Unexpected things happen more often than those you hope for.

UNHAPPY

Men who are unhappy, like men who sleep badly, are always proud of the fact.
—*Bertrand Russell*

UNICORNS

Never play leapfrog with a unicorn.

UNITED STATES

The United States never lost a war or won a conference.
—*Will Rogers*

UNIVERSE

I'm astounded by people who want to "know" the universe when it's hard enough to find your way around town.

UNKNOWN

People are afraid of the future, of the unknown.
If a man faces up to it and takes the dare of the
future, he can have some control over his destiny.
That's an exciting idea to me, better than waiting
with everybody else to see what's going to happen.
—*John Glenn*

USELESS

He is useless on top of the ground; he ought to be
under it, inspiring the cabbages.
—*Mark Twain*

VARIETY

It's a long road that has no turning.

VEGETARIANS

Vegetarians eat vegetables. What do humanitarians eat?

VICE PRESIDENT

The vice presidency is sort of like the last cookie on the plate. Everybody insists he won't take it, but somebody always does.
—*Bill Vaughan*

Once there were two brothers. One ran away to sea, and the other was elected vice president, and nothing was heard of either of them again.
—*Thomas Riley Marshall*

The vice president is like a man in a cataleptic state: He cannot speak; he cannot move; he suffers no pain; and yet he is perfectly conscious of everything that is going on around him.
—*Thomas Riley Marshall*

VILLAINY

One may smile and smile and be a villain.
—*William Shakespeare*

VOICEMAIL

You have reached the ———— family. What you hear is the barking of our killer Doberman pinscher, Wolf. Please leave a message after the tone.

VOTING

It's easier to vote a straight party ticket than it is to find a straight party.

Vote for the man who promises least; he'll be the least disappointing.
—*Bernard Baruch*

WAITERS

When you go to a restaurant, choose a table near a waiter.

WAITING

There are two kinds of people in one's life—people whom one keeps waiting and the people for whom one waits.
—*S. N. Behrman*

WALLETS

An empty wallet is heavier to carry than a full one.

WARDROBE

The little girl of today starts school with a larger wardrobe than her grandmother had when she got married.

WASHINGTON, D. C.

Washington is the place where nobody believes in rumor until it has been officially denied.

I love to go to Washington—if only to be near my money.
—*Bob Hope*

WEALTH

It is true that wealth won't make a man virtuous, but I notice there ain't anybody who wants to be poor just for the purpose of being good.
—*Josh Billings*

Anyone can become wealthy in America by inventing something useful that doesn't last long—like most home appliances.

WELL-ADJUSTED PEOPLE

A well-adjusted person is one who can play golf and bridge as if they were games.

WHEN . . .

When in doubt, mumble; when in trouble, delegate; when in charge, ponder.
—*James H. Boren*

WICKED

The wicked flee when no man pursueth, but they flee even faster when someone is after them.

WILL

Where there's a will there are relatives.

WINE

Wine hath drowned more men than the sea.
—*Thomas Fuller*

WINNERS

It's easy to spot winners—they're the ones not complaining about the rules.

WISDOM

The older I grow the more I distrust the familiar doctrine that age brings wisdom.
—*H. L. Mencken*

Not all things have to be scrutinized nor all friends tested nor all enemies exposed and denounced.

Nine-tenths of wisdom is being wise in time.
—*Theodore Roosevelt*

A wise man sees as much as he ought, not as much as he can.
—*Michel de Montaigne*

A wise man's question contains half the answer.

Fools live to regret their words, wise men to regret their silences.
—*Will Henry*

WISECRACKING

Wit has truth in it; wisecracking is simply calis-
thenics with words.
—*Dorothy Parker*

WISHES

Wishes won't do dishes.

If wishes were horses, beggars might ride.
—*John Ray*

WIT

Impropriety is the soul of wit.
—*W. Somerset Maugham*

Wit makes its own welcome and levels all distinc-
tions. No dignity, no learning, no force of character can make any stand against good wit.
—*Ralph Waldo Emerson*

Wit is the salt of conversation, not the food.
—*William Hazlitt*

WIVES

She would have made a splendid wife, for crying
only made her eyes more bright and tender.
—*O. Henry*

Any man who can't stand his wife lecturing to him
might find it a little easier to take sitting down.
—*Irvin S. Cobb*

Every man needs a wife because he can't blame everything on the government.

WOLVES

Many a father spends part of his time keeping the wolf from his door and the rest of the time keeping the wolf from his daughter.

It is useless for the sheep to pass resolutions in favor of vegetarianism while the wolf remains of a different opinion.
—*William Ralph Inge*

WOMAN'S INTUITION

What passes for woman's intuition is often nothing more than man's transparency.
—*George Jean Nathan*

WOMEN

Woman begins by resisting a man's advances and ends by blocking his retreat.
—*Oscar Wilde*

Not ten yoke of oxen have the power to draw us like a woman's hair!
—*Henry Wadsworth Longfellow*

On one issue at least, men and women agree: They both distrust women.
—*H. L. Mencken*

I hate women because they always know where things are.
—*James Thurber*

When a man boasts that he understands women, you can be sure that some woman has been flattering him.

Women don't dress to please men; if they did, they would dress a lot faster.

After equality, wage parity, liberation of body and soul, and the extension for the ratification of the ERA, women still can't do the following:
    Start barbecue fires
    Hook up a stereo
    Shine shoes
    Anything on a roof
    Decide where to hang a picture
    Investigate mysterious house noises at night

WOODPECKERS

Even the woodpecker owes his success to the fact that he uses his head and keeps pecking away until he finishes the job he starts.
—*Coleman Cox*

WORDS

Keep your words soft and sweet—you never know when you might have to eat them.

He can compress the most words into the smallest ideas of any man I ever met.
—*Abraham Lincoln*

Man does not live by words alone, despite the fact that sometimes he has to eat them.
—*Adlai Stevenson*

As long as words are in your mouth, you are their lord; once you utter them, you are their slave.
—*Solomon Ibn Gabirol*

The bitterest words are those we are forced to eat.

The longest word in the English language is the one following the phrase "And now a word from our sponsor."

WORK

Menial work brings out the disposition of people: Some turn up their sleeves, some turn up their noses, while most don't even turn up at all.

You'll never plough a field by turning it over in your mind.

I like work; it fascinates me. I can sit and look at it for hours. The idea of getting rid of it nearly breaks my heart.
—*Jerome K. Jerome*

Many a man works hard and saves money so that his sons won't have the disadvantages that made a man of their father.

My father taught me to work; he did not teach me to love it.
—*Abraham Lincoln*

All work and no play makes Jack the wealthiest man in the cemetery.

Anybody can do any amount of work, so long as it isn't the work he is supposed to be doing.
—*Robert Benchley*

Don't stand around doing nothing—people will think you're just a workman.

Don't stand around doing nothing—people will think you're the boss.

You can't occupy a place in the sun without being exposed to blisters.

Not to teach your son to work is like teaching him to steal.

WORKING OUT
I'm not into working out. My philosophy: No pain, no pain.
—*Carol Leifer*

WORRY

The reason worry kills more people than work is that more people worry than work.
—*Robert Frost*

Worry is like a rocking chair: Both give you something to do, but neither gets you anywhere.

Worry: the interest paid by those who borrow trouble.
—*George W. Lyon*

WRITERS

In the Soviet Union a writer who is critical, as we know, is taken to a lunatic asylum. In the United States he's taken to a talk show.
—*Carlos Fuentes*

WRITING

Some day I hope to write a book where the royalties will pay for the copies I give away.
—*Clarence Darrow*

Write—if you find work.

Every writer is a frustrated actor who recites his lines in the hidden auditorium of his skull.
—*Rod Serling*

He's a writer for the ages—for the ages of four to eight.
—*Dorothy Parker*

If you give me six lines written by the most honest man, I will find something in them to hang him.
—*Cardinal Richelieu*

The multitude of books is a great evil. There is no limit to this fever for writing.
—*Martin Luther*

When something can be read without effort, great effort has gone into its writing.
—*Enrique Jardiel Poncela*

After being turned down by numerous publishers, he decided to write for posterity.
—*George Ade*

Writing a book is an adventure: It begins as an amusement, then it becomes a mistress, then a master, and finally a tyrant.
—*Winston Churchill*

Writing is not hard. Just get paper and pencil, sit down, and write it as it occurs to you. The writing is easy—it's the occurring that's hard.
—*Stephen Leacock*

Writing is easy. All you do is stare at a blank sheet of paper until drops of blood form on your forehead.
—*Gene Fowler*

As a general rule, run your pen through every
other word you have written; you have no idea
what vigor it will give your style.
—*Sidney Smith*

The greatest part of a writer's time is spent in
reading in order to write; a man will turn over
half a library to make one book.
—*Samuel Johnson*

Make 'em laugh; make 'em cry; make 'em wait.
—*Charles Reade*

There's nothing to writing. All you do is sit down
at a typewriter and open a vein.
—*Red Smith*

His books are selling like wildfire. Everybody's
burning them.
—*George DeWitt*

WRONG

If you are willing to admit when you are wrong,
you are right.

The worst-tempered people I've ever met were
people who knew they were wrong.
—*Wilson Mizner*

If there is a wrong way to do something, then
someone will do it.
—*Edward A. Murphy*

YAWNS

A yawn is nature's way of giving the person listening to a bore an opportunity to open his mouth.

YOU'RE RIGHT

No sound is more pleasing to the human ear than the sound of someone admitting that you're right.

YOUTH

I am not young enough to know everything.
—*James M. Barrie*

I'll tell ya how to stay young: Hang around with older people.
—*Bob Hope*

The secret of staying young is to live honestly, eat slowly, and lie about your age.
—*Lucille Ball*

In America the young are always ready to give to those who are older than themselves the full benefits of their inexperience.
—*Oscar Wilde*

Youngsters brighten up a home, but only because they never turn off the lights.

The denunciation of the young is a necessary part of the hygiene of older people and greatly assists the circulation of their blood.
—*Logan Pearsall Smith*

YOUTHFUL FIGURES

A youthful figure is what you get when you ask a woman her age.

OTHER BOOKS BY BOB PHILLIPS

World's Greatest Collection of Clean Jokes
More Good Clean Jokes
The Last of the Good Clean Jokes
The Return of the Good Clean Jokes
The All-American Joke Book
The World's Greatest Collection of Heavenly Humor
The World's Greatest Collection of Riddles and
   Daffy Definitions
The World's Greatest Collection of Knock-Knock Jokes
   and Tongue Twisters
The Best of the Good Clean Jokes
Wit and Wisdom
Humor Is Tremendous
The All-New Clean Joke Book
Good Clean Jokes for Kids
The Encyclopedia of Clean Jokes
Bible Fun
Heavenly Fun
In Search of Bible Trivia, Vol. 1
In Search of Bible Trivia, Vol. 2
The Little Book of Bible Trivia

For information about how to purchase any of the above
books, please contact your local Christian bookstore.